AUSTIN DOBSON

SELECTED POEMS

Geo H Boughton.

Love in Winter

AUSTIN DOBSON

SELECTED POEMS

(REVISED AND ENLARGED EDITION)

GREENWOOD PRESS, PUBLISHERS
WESTPORT, CONNECTICUT

The Library of Congress has catalogued this publication as follows:

Library of Congress Cataloging in Publication Data

Dobson, Austin, 1840-1921.
   Selected poems.

   Original ed. issued as no. 249 of The World's
classics.
PR4606.A4 1972   821'.8   77-112323
ISBN 0-8371-4711-5

HENRY AUSTIN DOBSON, LL D.

Born, Plymouth .	.	. 18 Jan. 1840
Died, Ealing .	.	. 2 Sept. 1921

Originally published in 1924
by Oxford University Press, London

Reprinted with the permission
of Oxford University Press

First Greenwood Reprinting 1972

Library of Congress Catalogue Card Number 77-112323

ISBN 0-8371-4711-5

Printed in the United States of America

PREFACE

THE forerunner of the present edition of *Selected Poems* was published by Messrs. Kegan Paul, Trench, Trübner & Co., Ltd., in their *Dryden Library*, in 1905. It was reprinted in 1909, and the residue of that edition was transferred to, and issued by the Oxford University Press, in the *World's Classics* Series, in 1923. The exhaustion of that edition affords a suitable opportunity for issuing a selected edition completely representative of the Author's Poetical Works.

The identical editions of 1905 and 1909 consisted of fifty-one poems, selected by the Author himself, and were based on a comparatively early edition of his *Collected Poems*, issued by the Publishers first above mentioned.

The present edition, which may be re-garded as the final edition of *Selected Poems*, contains all the poems appearing in the previous issues, and some thirty-seven poems in addition. It is based on the Author's *Complete Poetical Works*, published by the Oxford University Press in December 1923, and contains roughly one-quarter of the poems comprised in that volume.

The poems follow the same order as in the *Complete Poetical Works*, and the *Contents* page shows the various sections of that volume from which they have been selected. At the foot of each poem is inserted the date of its first appearance in print. When the date of its composition is known to have been earlier, that date is also shown in brackets. In view of the very full notes appended to the complete edition, no notes are included in the present volume.

The pen and ink drawing made by the late G. H. Boughton, R. A., in the Poet's own copy of *At the Sign of the Lyre*, to illustrate the poem *Love in Winter* (see p. 65) is again re-produced as a frontispiece.

Quot homines, tot sententiae is eminently

true of Austin Dobson's poems. If therefore the present selection, for which I must take full responsibility, fails to satisfy all those who take up this little volume, I can only hope that they will have recourse to the complete volume of the Author's Poetry, to which previous reference has been made.

ALBAN DOBSON.

EALING, 1924.

CONTENTS

*T*O you I sing, whom towns immure,
  And bonds of toil hold fast and sure ;—
    To you across whose aching sight
    Come woodlands bathed in April light,
And dreams of pastime premature.

And you, O Sad, who still endure
Some wound that only Time can cure,—
    To you, in watches of the night,—
            To you I sing !

But most to you with eyelids pure,
Scarce witting yet of love or lure ;—
    To you, with bird-like glances bright,
    Half-paused to speak, half-poised in flight ;
O English Girl, divine, demure,
            To YOU I sing !

  1876.

A DEAD LETTER

" À cœur blessé—l'ombre et le silence.
—H. DE BALZAC.

I

I DREW it from its china tomb ;—
  It came out feebly scented
With some thin ghost of past perfume
  That dust and days had lent it.

An old, old letter,—folded still !
  To read with due composure,
I sought the sun-lit window-sill,
  Above the gray enclosure,

That glimmering in the sultry haze,
  Faint-flowered, dimly shaded,
Slumbered like Goldsmith's Madam Blaize,
  Bedizened and brocaded.

A queer old place !   You'd surely say
  Some tea-board garden-maker
Had planned it in Dutch William's day
  To please some florist Quaker,

So trim it was.   The yew-trees still,
　With pious care perverted,
Grew in the same grim shapes; and still
　The lipless dolphin spurted;

Still in his wonted state abode
　The broken-nosed Apollo;
And still the cypress-arbour showed
　The same umbrageous hollow.

Only,—as fresh young Beauty gleams
　From coffee-coloured laces,—
So peeped from its old-fashioned dreams
　The fresher modern traces;

For idle mallet, hoop, and ball
　Upon the lawn were lying;
A magazine, a tumbled shawl,
　Round which the swifts were flying;

And, tossed beside the Guelder rose,
　A heap of rainbow knitting,
Where, blinking in her pleased repose,
　A Persian cat was sitting.

"A place to love in,—live,—for aye,
　　If we too, like Tithonus,
Could find some God to stretch the gray,
　　Scant life the Fates have thrown us ;

"But now by steam we run our race,
　　With buttoned heart and pocket ;
Our Love's a gilded, surplus grace,—
　　Just like an empty locket !

"'The time is out of joint.'　Who will,
　　May strive to make it better ;
For me, this warm old window-sill,
　　And this old dusty letter."

II

"Dear *John* (the letter ran), it can't, can't be,
　　For Father's gone to *Chorley Fair* with *Sam*,
And Mother's storing Apples,—*Prue* and me
　　Up to our Elbows making Damson Jam :
But we shall meet before a Week is gone,—
''Tis a long Lane that has no turning,' *John !*

"Only till Sunday next, and then you'll wait
  Behind the White-Thorn, by the broken
    Stile—
We can go round and catch them at the Gate,
  All to Ourselves, for nearly one long Mile;
Dear *Prue* won't look, and Father he'll go on,
And *Sam's* two Eyes are all for *Cissy, John!*

"*John*, she's so smart,—with every Ribbon new,
  Flame-coloured Sack, and Crimson Padesoy:
As proud as proud; and has the Vapours too,
  Just like My Lady;—calls poor *Sam* a Boy,
And vows no Sweet-heart's worth the Thinking-
    on
Till he's past Thirty . . . I know better, *John!*

"My Dear, I don't think that I thought of much
  Before we knew each other, I and you;
And now, why, *John*, your least, least Finger-
    touch,
  Gives me enough to think a Summer through.
See, for I send you Something! There, 'tis
    gone!
Look in this corner,—mind you find it, *John!*

III

This was the matter of the note·—
  A long-forgot deposit,
Dropped in an Indian dragon's throat,
  Deep in a fragrant closet,

Piled with a dapper Dresden world,—
  Beaux, beauties, prayers, and poses,—
Bonzes with squat legs undercurled,
  And great jars filled with roses.

Ah, heart that wrote !   Ah, lips that kissed !
  You had no thought or presage
Into what keeping you dismissed
  Your simple old-world message !

A reverent one.   Though we to-day
  Distrust beliefs and powers,
The artless, ageless things you say
  Are fresh as May's own flowers,

Starring some pure, primeval spring,
  Ere Gold had grown despotic,—
Ere life was yet a selfish thing,
  Or Love a mere exotic !

I need not search too much to find
  Whose lot it was to send it,
That feel upon me yet the kind,
  Soft hand of her who penned it;

And see, through two score years of smoke,
  In by-gone, quaint apparel,
Shine from yon time-black Norway oak
  The face of Patience Caryl,—

The pale, smooth forehead, silver-tressed;
  The gray gown, primly flowered;
The spotless, stately coif whose crest
  Like Hector's horse-plume towered;

And still the sweet half-solemn look,
  Where some past thought was clinging,
As when one shuts a serious book
  To hear the thrushes singing.

I kneel to you!   Of those you were,
  Whose kind old hearts grow mellow,—
Whose fair old faces grow more fair
  As Point and Flanders yellow;

Whom some old store of garnered grief,
  Their placid temples shading,
Crowns like a wreath of autumn leaf
  With tender tints of fading.

Peace to your soul! You died unwed—
  Despite this loving letter.
And what of John? The less that's said
  Of John, I think, the better.

1868.

A GENTLEMAN OF THE OLD SCHOOL

HE lived in that past Georgian day,
　　When men were less inclined to say
That "Time is Gold," and overlay
　　　　With toil their pleasure ;
He held some land, and dwelt thereon,—
Where, I forget,—the house is gone ;
His Christian name, I think, was John,—
　　　　His surname, Leisure.

Reynolds has painted him,—a face
Filled with a fine, old-fashioned grace,
Fresh-coloured, frank, with ne'er a trace
　　　　Of trouble shaded ;
The eyes are blue, the hair is drest
In plainest way,—one hand is prest
Deep in a flapped canary vest,
　　　　With buds brocaded.

He wears a brown old Brunswick coat,
With silver buttons,—round his throat,
A soft cravat ;—in all you note
        An elder fashion,—
A strangeness, which, to us who shine
In shapely hats,—whose coats combine
All harmonies of hue and line,—
        Inspires compassion.

He lived so long ago, you see !
Men were untravelled then, but we,
Like Ariel, post o'er land and sea
        With careless parting ;
He found it quite enough for him
To smoke his pipe in " garden trim,"
And watch, about the fish-tank's brim,
        The swallows darting.

He liked the well-wheel's creaking tongue,—
He liked the thrush that stopped and sung,—
He liked the drone of flies among
        His netted peaches ;
He liked to watch the sunlight fall
Athwart his ivied orchard wall ;
Or pause to catch the cuckoo's call
        Beyond the beeches.

His were the times of Paint and Patch,
And yet no Ranelagh could match
The sober doves that round his thatch
        Spread tails and sidled ;
He liked their ruffling, puffed content,—
For him their drowsy wheelings meant
More than a Mall of Beaux that bent,
        Or Belles that bridled.

Not that, in truth, when life began,
He shunned the flutter of the fan ;
He too had maybe "pinked his man"
        In Beauty's quarrel ;
But now his "fervent youth" had flown
Where lost things go ; and he was grown
As staid and slow-paced as his own
        Old hunter, Sorrel.

Yet still he loved the chase, and held
That no composer's score excelled
The merry horn, when Sweetlip swelled
        Its jovial riot ;
But most his measured words of praise
Caressed the angler's easy ways,—
His idly meditative days,—
        His rustic diet.

Not that his "meditating" rose
Beyond a sunny summer doze ;
He never troubled his repose
   With fruitless prying ;
But held, as law for high and low,
What God withholds no man can know,
And smiled away inquiry so,
   Without replying.

We read—alas, how much we read !
The jumbled strifes of creed and creed
With endless controversies feed
   Our groaning tables ;
His books—and they sufficed him—were
Cotton's " Montaigne," "The Grave" of Blair
A "Walton"—much the worse for wear—
   And " Æsop's Fables."

One more,—" The Bible."   Not that he
Had searched its page as deep as we ;
No sophistries could make him see
   Its slender credit ;
It may be that he could not count
The sires and sons to Jesse's fount,—
He liked the " Sermon on the Mount,"—
   And more, he read it.

Once he had loved, but failed to wed,
A red-cheeked lass who long was dead ;
His ways were far too slow, he said,
        To quite forget her ;
And still when time had turned him gray,
The earliest hawthorn-buds in May
Would find his lingering feet astray,
        Where first he met her.

"*In Cœlo Quies*" heads the stone
On Leisure's grave,—now little known,
A tangle of wild-rose has grown
        So thick across it ;
The "Benefactions" still declare
He left the clerk an elbow-chair,
And "12 Pence Yearly to Prepare
        A Christmas Posset."

Lie softly, Leisure !   Doubtless you
With too serene a conscience drew
Your easy breath, and slumbered through
        The gravest issue ;
But we, to whom our age allows
Scarce space to wipe our weary brows,
Look down upon your narrow house,
        Old Friend, and miss you.

1870.

A GENTLEWOMAN OF THE OLD SCHOOL

SHE lived in Georgian era too.
  Most women then, if bards be true,
Succumbed to Routs and Cards, or grew
      Devout and acid.
But hers was neither fate. She came
Of good west-country folk, whose fame
Has faded now. For us her name
      Is " Madam Placid."

Patience or Prudence,—what you will,
Some prefix faintly fragrant still
As those old musky scents that fill
      Our grandams' pillows ;
And for her youthful portrait take
Some long-waist child of Hudson's make,
Stiffly at ease beside a lake
      With swans and willows.

I keep her later semblance placed
Beside my desk,—'tis lawned and laced,
In shadowy sanguine stipple traced
        By Bartolozzi ;
A placid face, in which surprise
Is seldom seen, but yet there lies
Some vestige of the laughing eyes
        Of arch Piozzi.

For her e'en Time grew debonair.
He, finding cheeks unclaimed of care,
With late-delayed faint roses there,
        And lingering dimples,
Had spared to touch the fair old face,
And only kissed with Vauxhall grace
The soft white hand that stroked her lace,
        Or smoothed her wimples.

So left her beautiful.   Her age
Was comely as her youth was sage,
And yet she once had been the rage ;—
        It hath been hinted,
Indeed, affirmed by one or two,
Some spark at Bath (as sparks will do)
Inscribed a song to " Lovely Prue,"
        Which Urban printed.

I know she thought ; I know she felt ;
Perchance could sum, I doubt she spelt ;
She knew as little of the Celt
          As of the Saxon ;
I know she played and sang, for yet
We keep the tumble-down spinet
To which she quavered ballads set
          By Arne or Jackson.

Her tastes were not refined as ours ;
She liked plain food and homely flowers,
Refused to paint, kept early hours,
          Went clad demurely ;
Her art was sampler-work design,
Fireworks for her were "vastly fine,"
Her luxury was elder-wine,—
          She loved that "purely."

She was renowned, traditions say,
For June conserves, for curds and whey,
For finest tea (she called it "tay"),
          And ratafia ;
She knew, for sprains, what bands to choose,
Could tell the sovereign wash to use
For freckles, and was learned in brews
          As erst Medea.

Yet studied little.   She would read,
On Sundays, "Pearson on the Creed,"
Though, as I think, she could not heed
       His text profoundly ;
Seeing she chose for her retreat
The warm west-looking window-seat,
Where, if you chanced to raise your feet,
       You slumbered soundly.

This, 'twixt ourselves.   The dear old dame,
In truth, was not so much to blame ;
The excellent divine I name
       Is scarcely stirring ;
Her plain-song piety preferred
Pure life to precept.   If she erred,
She knew her faults.   Her softest word
       Was for the erring.

If she had loved, or if she kept
Some ancient memory green, or wept
Over the shoulder-knot that slept
       Within her cuff-box,
I know not.   Only this I know,
At sixty-five she'd still her beau,
A lean French exile, lame and slow,
       With monstrous snuff-box.

Younger than she, well-born and bred.
She'd found him in St. Giles', half dead
Of teaching French for nightly bed
       And daily dinners :
Starving, in fact, 'twixt want and pride ;
And so, henceforth, you always spied
His rusty "pigeon-wings" beside
       Her Mechlin pinners.

He worshipped her, you may suppose.
She gained him pupils, gave him clothes,
Delighted in his dry bons mots
       And cackling laughter ;
And when, at last, the long duet
Of conversation and piquet
Ceased with her death, of sheer regret
       He died soon after.

Dear Madam Placid !   Others knew
Your worth as well as he, and threw
Their flowers upon your coffin too,
       I take for granted.
Their loves are lost ; but still we see
Your kind and gracious memory
Bloom yearly with the almond tree
       The Frenchman planted.

1871.

THE BALLAD OF "BEAU BROCADE"

"Hark! I hear the sound of coaches!"
—BEGGAR'S OPERA.

SEVENTEEN hundred and thirty-nine :—
That was the date of this tale of mine.

First great GEORGE was buried and gone ;
GEORGE the Second was plodding on.

LONDON then, as the " Guides " aver,
Shared its glories with *Westminster;*

And people of rank, to correct their " tone,"
Went out of town to *Marybone.*

Those were the days of the War with *Spain,*
PORTO-BELLO would soon be ta'en ;

WHITEFIELD preached to the colliers grim,
Bishops in lawn sleeves preached at him ;

WALPOLE talked of "a man and his price";
Nobody's virtue was over-nice :—

Those, in fine, were the brave days when
Coaches were stopped by . . *Highwaymen!*

And of all the knights of the gentle trade
Nobody bolder than "BEAU BROCADE."

This they knew on the whole way down;
Best,—maybe,—at the "*Oak and Crown.*"

(For timorous cits on their pilgrimage
Would "club" for a "Guard" to ride the stage;

And the Guard that rode on more than one
Was the Host of this hostel's sister's son.)

Open we here on a March day fine,
Under the oak with the hanging sign.

There was Barber DICK with his basin by;
Cobbler JOE with the patch on his eye;

Portly product of Beef and Beer,
JOHN the host, he was standing near.

Straining and creaking, with wheels awry,
Lumbering came the "*Plymouth Fly*";—

Lumbering up from *Bagshot Heath*,
Guard in the basket armed to the teeth;

Passengers heavily armed inside;
Not the less surely the coach had been tried!

Tried!—but a couple of miles away,
By a well-dressed man!—in the open day!

Tried successfully, never a doubt,—
Pockets of passengers all turned out!

Cloak-bags rifled, and cushions ripped,—
Even an Ensign's wallet stripped!

Even a Methodist hosier's wife
Offered the choice of her Money or Life!

Highwayman's manners no less polite,
Hoped that their coppers (returned) were
    right;—

Sorry to find the company poor,
Hoped next time they'd travel with more;—

Plucked them all at his ease, in short :—
Such was the "*Plymouth Fly's*" report.

Sympathy ! horror ! and wonderment !
"Catch the Villain !"   (But Nobody went.)

Hosier's wife led into the Bar ;
(That's where the best strong waters are !)

Followed the tale of the hundred-and-one
Things that Somebody ought to have done.

Ensign (of BRAGG'S) made a terrible clangour :
But for the Ladies had drawn his hanger !

Robber, of course, was "BEAU BROCADE" ;
Out-spoke DOLLY the Chambermaid.

Devonshire DOLLY, plump and red,
Spoke from the gallery overhead ;—

Spoke it out boldly, staring hard :—
"Why didn't you shoot then, GEORGE the
    Guard ?"

Spoke it out bolder, seeing him mute :—
"GEORGE the Guard, why didn't you shoot ?"

Portly JOHN grew pale and red,
(JOHN was afraid of her, people said ;)

Gasped that "DOLLY was surely cracked,"
(JOHN was afraid of her—that's a fact !)

GEORGE the Guard grew red and pale,
Slowly finished his quart of ale :—

"Shoot?   Why — Rabbit him ! — didn't he
    shoot ?"
Muttered—"The Baggage was far too 'cute ! "

"Shoot?   Why he'd flashed the pan in his
    eye !"
Muttered—"She'd pay for it by and by !"
Further than this made no reply.

Nor could a further reply be made,
For GEORGE *was in league with* "BEAU
    BROCADE" !

And JOHN the Host, in his wakefullest state,
Was not—on the whole—immaculate.

But nobody's virtue was over-nice
When WALPOLE talked of "a man and his
    price";

And wherever Purity found abode,
'Twas certainly *not* on a posting road.

II

"Forty" followed to "Thirty-nine."
Glorious days of the *Hanover* line!

Princes were born, and drums were banged;
Now and then batches of Highwaymen hanged.

"Glorious news!"—from the *Spanish Main;*
PORTO-BELLO at last was ta'en.

"Glorious news!"—for the liquor trade;
Nobody dreamed of "BEAU BROCADE."

People were thinking of *Spanish Crowns;*
Money was coming from sea-port towns!

Nobody dreamed of " BEAU BROCADE,"
(Only DOLLY the Chambermaid !)

Blessings on VERNON !   Fill up the cans ;
Money was coming in " *Flys* " and " *Vans.*"

Possibly JOHN the Host had heard ;
Also, certainly, GEORGE the Guard.

And DOLLY had possibly tidings, too,
That made her rise from her bed anew,

Plump as ever, but stern of eye,
With a fixed intention to warn the " *Fly.*"

Lingering only at JOHN his door,
Just to make sure of a jerky snore ;

Saddling the gray mare, *Dumpling Star ;*
Fetching the pistol out of the bar ;

(The old horse-pistol that, they say,
Came from the battle of *Malplaquet ;*)

Loading with powder that maids would use,
Even in " Forty," to clear the flues ;

And a couple of silver buttons, the Squire
Gave her, away in *Devonshire.*

These she wadded—for want of better—
With the B—SH—P of L—ND—N'S "Pastoral
    Letter";

Looked to the flint, and hung the whole,
Ready to use, at her pocket-hole.

Thus equipped and accoutred, DOLLY
Clattered away to "*Exciseman's Folly*";—

Such was the name of a ruined abode,
Just on the edge of the *London* road.

Thence she thought she might safely try,
As soon as she saw it, to warn the "*Fly.*"

But, as chance fell out, her rein she drew,
As the BEAU came cantering into the view.

By the light of the moon she could see him drest
In his famous gold-sprigged tambour vest;

And under his silver-gray surtout,
The laced, historical coat of blue,

That he wore when he went to *London-Spaw*,
And robbed Sir MUNGO MUCKLETHRAW.

Out-spoke DOLLY the Chambermaid,
(Trembling a little, but not afraid,)
"Stand and Deliver, O 'BEAU BROCADE'!"

But the BEAU rode nearer, and would not speak,
For he saw by the moonlight a rosy cheek;

And a spavined mare with a rusty hide;
And a girl with her hand at her pocket-side.

So never a word he spoke as yet,
For he thought 'twas a freak of MEG or BET;—
A freak of the "*Rose*" or the "*Rummer*" set.

Out-spoke DOLLY the Chambermaid,
(Tremulous now, and sore afraid,)
"Stand and Deliver, O 'BEAU BROCADE'!"—

Firing then, out of sheer alarm,
Hit the BEAU in the bridle-arm.

Button the first went none knows where,
But it carried away his *solitaire;*

Button the second a circuit made,
Glanced in under the shoulder-blade ;—
Down from the saddle fell "BEAU BROCADE"!

Down from the saddle and never stirred !—
DOLLY grew white as a *Windsor* curd.

Slipped not less from the mare, and bound
Strips of her kirtle about his wound.

Then, lest his Worship should rise and flee,
Fettered his ankles—tenderly.

Jumped on his chestnut, BET the fleet
(Called after BET of *Portugal Street*) ;

Came like the wind to the old Inn-door ;—
Roused fat JOHN from a three-fold snore ;—

Vowed she'd 'peach if he misbehaved . . .
Briefly, the "*Plymouth Fly*" was saved !

Staines and *Windsor* were all on fire :—
DOLLY was wed to a *Yorkshire* squire ;
Went to Town at the K—G's desire !

But whether His M—J—STY saw her or not,
HOGARTH jotted her down on the spot;

And something of DOLLY one still may trace
In the fresh contours of his "*Milkmaid's*" face.

GEORGE the Guard fled over the sea:
JOHN had a fit—of perplexity;

Turned King's evidence, sad to state;—
But JOHN was never immaculate.

As for the BEAU, he was duly tried,
When his wound was healed, at *Whitsuntide;*

Served—for a day—as the last of "sights,"
To the world of *St. James's-Street* and "*White's,*"

Went on his way to TYBURN TREE,
With a pomp befitting his high degree.

Every privilege rank confers:—
Bouquet of pinks at *St. Sepulchre's;*

Flagon of ale at *Holborn Bar;*
Friends (in mourning) to follow his Car—
("t" is omitted where HEROES are!)

Every one knows the speech he made ;
Swore that he "rather admired the Jade !"—

Waved to the crowd with his gold-laced hat :
Talked to the Chaplain after that ;

Turned to the Topsman undismayed . . .
This was the finish of "BEAU BROCADE" !

*And this is the Ballad that seemed to hide
In the leaves of a dusty "LONDONER'S GUIDE" ;*

*" Humbly Inscrib'd (with curls and tails)
By the Author, to* FREDERICK, *Prince of*
     WALES :—

" Published by FRANCIS *and* OLIVER PINE ;
*Ludgate-Hill, at the Blackmoor Sign.
Seventeen-Hundred-and-Forty-Nine."*

  1876.

UNE MARQUISE

A RHYMED MONOLOGUE IN THE LOUVRE

"Belle Marquise, vos beaux yeux me font mourir d'amour."—MOLIÈRE.

I

AS you sit there at your ease,
   O Marquise!
And the men flock round your knees
   Thick as bees,
Mute at every word you utter,
Servants to your least frill-flutter,
   "Belle Marquise!"—
As you sit there growing prouder,
 And your ringed hands glance and go,
And your fan's *frou-frou* sounds louder,
 And your *"beaux yeux"* flash and glow ;—
Ah, you used them on the Painter,
   As you know,

For the Sieur Larose spoke fainter,
                Bowing low,
Thanked Madame and Heaven for mercy
That each sitter was not Circe,
  Or at least he told you so ;—
Growing proud, I say, and prouder
  To the crowd that come and go,
Dainty Deity of Powder,
  Fickle Queen of Fop and Beau,
As you sit where lustres strike you,
                Sure to please,
Do we love you most, or like you,
              " Belle Marquise ? "

II

You are fair ; O yes, we know it
                Well, Marquise :
For he swore it, your last poet,
                On his knees ;
And he called all heaven to witness
Of his ballad and its fitness,
              " Belle Marquise ! "—
You were everything in *ère*
(With exception of *sévère*),—

You were *cruelle* and *rebelle*,
With the rest of rhymes as well;
You were "*Reine*," and "*Mère d'Amour*";
   You were "*Vénus à Cythère*";
"*Sappho mise en Pompadour*,"
   And "*Minerve en Parabère*";
You had every grace of heaven
   In your most angelic face,
With the nameless finer leaven
   Lent of blood and courtly race;
And he added, too, in duty,
Ninon's wit and Boufflers' beauty;
And La Vallière's *yeux veloutés*
            Followed these;
And you liked it, when he said it
            (On his knees),
And you kept it, and you read it,
        "*Belle Marquise!*"

III

Yet with us your toilet graces
           Fail to please,
And the last of your last faces,
           And your *mise;*
  For we hold you just as real,
        "*Belle Marquise!*"

As your *Bergers* and *Bergères*,
Iles d'Amour and *Batelières;*
As your *parcs*, and your Versailles,
Gardens, grottoes, and *rocailles;*
As your Naiads and your trees ;—
   Just as near the old ideal
               Calm and ease,
As the Venus there, by Coustou,
   That a fan would make quite flighty,
Is to her the gods were used to,—
   Is to grand Greek Aphroditè,
            Sprung from seas.
You are just a porcelain trifle,
      " Belle Marquise !"
Just a thing of puffs and patches,
Made for madrigals and catches,
Not for heart-wounds, but for scratches,
        O Marquise !
Just a pinky porcelain trifle,
      " Belle Marquise !"
Wrought in rarest *rose-Dubarry*,
Quick at verbal point and parry,
Clever, doubtless ;—but to marry,
        No, Marquise !

IV

For your Cupid, you have clipped him,
Rouged and patched him, nipped and snipped
    him,
And with *chapeau-bras* equipped him,
                 "*Belle Marquise!*"
Just to arm you through your wife-time,
And the languors of your life-time,
                 "*Belle Marquise!*"
Say, to trim your toilet tapers,
Or,—to twist your hair in papers,
Or,—to wean you from the vapours ;—
                 As for these,
You are worth the love they give you,
Till a fairer face outlive you,
  Or a younger grace shall please ;
Till the coming of the crows' feet,
And the backward turn of beaux' feet,
                 "*Belle Marquise!*"—
Till your frothed-out life's commotion
Settles down to Ennui's ocean,
Or a dainty sham devotion,
             "*Belle Marquise!*"

V

No : we neither like nor love you,
          " Belle Marquise!"
Lesser lights we place above you,—
   Milder merits better please.
We have passed from *Philosophe*-dom
   Into plainer modern days,—
Grown contented in our oafdom,
   Giving grace not all the praise ;
And, *en partant, Arsinoé,*—
   Without malice whatsoever,—
We shall counsel to our Chloë
   To be rather good than clever ;
For we find it hard to smother
   Just one little thought, Marquise !
Wittier perhaps than any other,—
You were neither Wife nor Mother,
          " Belle Marquise!"

1868.

"GOOD-NIGHT, BABETTE!"

" Si vieillesse pouvait !—"

SCENE.—*A small neat Room. In a high Voltaire
Chair sits a white-haired old Gentleman.*

MONSIEUR VIEUXBOIS.   BABETTE.

M. VIEUXBOIS (*turning querulously*).

DAY of my life ! Where *can* she get?
    BABETTE ! I say ! BABETTE !—BABETTE !

BABETTE (*entering hurriedly*).

Coming M'sieu' ! If M'sieu' speaks
So loud, he won't be well for weeks !

M. VIEUXBOIS.

Where have you been?

BABETTE.

        Why, M'sieu' knows :—
April ! . . . Ville d'Avray ! . . . Ma'am'selle Rose !

M. VIEUXBOIS.

Ah! I am old,—and I forget.
Was the place growing green, BABETTE?

BABETTE.

But of a greenness!—yes, M'sieu'!
And then the sky so blue!— so blue!
And when I dropped my *immortelle*,
How the birds sang!
> (*Lifting her apron to her eyes.*)
>> This poor Ma'am'selle!

M. VIEUXBOIS.

You're a good girl, BABETTE, but she,—
She was an Angel, verily.
Sometimes I think I see her yet
Stand smiling by the cabinet;
And once, I know, she peeped and laughed
Betwixt the curtains . . .
>> Where's the draught?

> (*She gives him a cup.*)

Now I shall sleep, I think, BABETTE;—
Sing me your Norman *chansonnette.*

BABETTE (*sings*).

" *Once at the Angelus*
  (Ere I was dead),
Angels all glorious
  Came to my Bed ;
Angels in blue and white
  Crowned on the Head."

M. VIEUXBOIS (*drowsily*)

" She was an Angel " .. " Once she laughed " ...
What, was I dreaming ?

           Where's the draught ?

BABETTE (*showing the empty cup*).

The draught, M'sieu' ?

M. VIEUXBOIS.

           How I forget !
I am so old !   But sing, BABETTE !

BABETTE (*sings*).

" *One was the Friend I left*
  Stark in the Snow ;
One was the Wife that died
  Long,—long ago ;
One was the Love I lost . . .
  How could she know ? "

M. VIEUXBOIS (*murmuring*).

Ah, PAUL ! . . . old PAUL ! . . . EULALIE too !
And ROSE . . . And O ! "the sky so blue ! "

BABETTE (*sings*).

" *One had my Mother's eyes,*
     Wistful and mild ;
   One had my Father's face ;
     One was a Child :
   All of them bent to me,—
     Bent down and smiled ! "

(He is asleep !)

M. VIEUXBOIS (*almost inaudibly*).

        " How I forget ! "
" I am so old ! " . . . " Good-night, BABETTE ! "

   1876.

THE DRAMA OF THE DOCTOR'S WINDOW

IN THREE ACTS, WITH A PROLOGUE

" *A tedious brief scene of young Pyramus,*
And his love Thisbe ; very tragical mirth."
—MIDSUMMER-NIGHT'S DREAM.

PROLOGUE.

" WELL, I must wait !" The Doctor's
          room,
    Where I used this expression,
Wore the severe official gloom
    Attached to that profession ;
Rendered severer by a bald
    And skinless Gladiator,
Whose raw robustness first appalled
    The entering spectator.

No one would call "The Lancet" gay,—
  Few could avoid confessing
That Jones, "On Muscular Decay,"
  Is—as a rule—depressing :
So, leaving both, to change the scene,
  I turned toward the shutter,
And peered out vacantly between
  A water-butt and gutter.

Below, the Doctor's garden lay,
  If thus imagination
May dignify a square of clay
  Unused to vegetation,
Filled with a dismal-looking swing—
  That brought to mind a gallows—
An empty kennel, mouldering,
  And two dyspeptic aloes.

No sparrow chirped, no daisy sprung,
  About the place deserted ;
Only across the swing-board hung
  A battered doll, inverted,
Which sadly seemed to disconcert
  The vagrant cat that scanned it,
Sniffed doubtfully around the skirt,
  But failed to understand it.

A dreary spot ! And yet, I own,
　Half hoping that, perchance, it
Might, in some unknown way, atone
　For Jones and for " The Lancet,"
I watched ; and by especial grace,
　Within this stage contracted,
Saw presently before my face
　A classic story acted.

Ah, World of ours, are you so gray
　And weary, World, of spinning,
That you repeat the tales to-day
　You told at the beginning ?
For lo ! the same old myths that made
　The early " stage successes,"
Still " hold the boards," and still are played,
　" With new effects and dresses."

Small, lonely " three-pair-backs " behold,
　To-day, Alcestis dying ;
To-day, in farthest Polar cold,
　Ulysses' bones are lying ;
Still in one's morning " Times " one reads
　How fell an Indian Hector ;
Still clubs discuss Achilles' steeds,
　Briseis' next protector ;—

Still Menelaus brings, we see,
　　His oft-remanded case on ;
Still somewhere sad Hypsipyle
　　Bewails a faithless Jason ;
And here, the Doctor's sill beside,
　　Do I not now discover
A Thisbe, whom the walls divide
　　From Pyramus, her lover?

ACT THE FIRST.

Act I. began.   Some noise had scared
　　The cat, that like an arrow
Shot up the wall and disappeared ;
　　And then, across the narrow,
Unweeded path, a small dark thing,
　　Hid by a garden-bonnet,
Passed wearily towards the swing,
　　Paused, turned, and climbed upon it.

A child of five, with eyes that were
　　At least a decade older,
A mournful mouth, and tangled hair
　　Flung careless round her shoulder,

Dressed in a stiff ill-fitting frock,
  Whose black, uncomely rigour
Sardonically seemed to mock
  The plaintive, slender figure.

What was it?   Something in the dress
  That told the girl unmothered ;
Or was it that the merciless
  Black garb of mourning smothered
Life and all light :—but rocking so,
  In the dull garden-corner,
The lonely swinger seemed to grow
  More piteous and forlorner.

Then, as I looked, across the wall
  Of "next-door's" garden, that is—
To speak correctly—through its tall
  Surmounting fence of lattice,
Peeped a boy's face, with curling hair,
  Ripe lips, half drawn asunder,
And round, bright eyes, that wore a stare
  Of frankest childish wonder.

Rounder they grew by slow degrees,
  Until the swinger, swerving,
Made, all at once, alive to these
  Intentest orbs observing,

Gave just one brief, half-uttered cry,
  And,—as with gathered kirtle,
Nymphs fly from Pan's head suddenly
  Thrust through the budding myrtle,—

Fled in dismay. A moment's space,
  The eyes looked almost tragic ;
Then, when they caught my watching face
  Vanished as if by magic ;
And, like some sombre thing beguiled
  To strange, unwonted laughter,
The gloomy garden, having smiled,
  Became the gloomier after.

ACT THE SECOND.

Yes : they were gone, the stage was bare,—
  Blank as before ; and therefore,
Sinking within the patient's chair,
  Half vexed, I knew not wherefore,
I dozed ; till, startled by some call,
  A glance sufficed to show me,
The boy again above the wall,
  The girl erect below me.

The boy, it seemed, to add a force
  To words found unavailing,
Had pushed a striped and spotted horse
  Half through the blistered paling,
Where now it stuck, stiff-legged and straight,
  While he, in exultation,
Chattered some half-articulate
  Excited explanation.

Meanwhile, the girl, with upturned face,
  Stood motionless, and listened ;
The ill-cut frock had gained a grace,
  The pale hair almost glistened ;
The figure looked alert and bright,
  Buoyant as though some power
Had lifted it, as rain at night
  Uplifts a drooping flower.

The eyes had lost their listless way,—
  The old life, tired and faded,
Had slipped down with the doll that lay
  Before her feet, degraded ;
She only, yearning upward, found
  In those bright eyes above her
The ghost of some enchanted ground
  Where even Nurse would love her.

Ah, tyrant Time ! you hold the book,
    We, sick and sad, begin it ;
You close it fast, if we but look
    Pleased for a meagre minute ;
You closed it now, for, out of sight,
    Some warning finger beckoned ;
Exeunt both to left and right ;—
    Thus ended Act the Second.

ACT THE THIRD.

Or so it proved.   For while I still
    Believed them gone for ever,
Half raised above the window sill,
    I saw the lattice quiver ;
And lo, once more appeared the head,
    Flushed, while the round mouth pouted ;
"Give Tom a kiss," the red lips said,
    In style the most undoubted.

The girl came back without a thought ;
    Dear Muse of Mayfair, pardon,
If more restraint had not been taught
    In this neglected garden ;

For these your code was all too stiff,
 So, seeing none dissented,
Their unfeigned faces met as if
 Manners were not invented.

Then on the scene,—by happy fate,
 When lip from lip had parted,
And, therefore, just two seconds late,—
 A sharp-faced nurse-maid darted ;
Swooped on the boy, as swoops a kite
 Upon a rover chicken,
And bore him sourly off, despite
 His well-directed kicking.

The girl stood silent, with a look
 Too subtle to unravel,
Then, with a sudden gesture took
 The torn doll from the gravel ;
Hid the whole face, with one caress,
 Under the garden-bonnet,
And, passing in, I saw her press
 Kiss after kiss upon it.

———

Exeunt omnes.   End of play.
 It made the dull room brighter,
The Gladiator almost gay,
 And e'en "The Lancet" lighter.
1870.

AN AUTUMN IDYLL

"Sweet Themmes! runne softly, till I end my song."
—SPENSER.

LAWRENCE.   FRANK.   JACK.

LAWRENCE.

HERE, where the beech-nuts drop among
    the grasses,
  Push the boat in, and throw the rope ashore.
Jack, hand me out the claret and the glasses ;
  Here let us sit.   We landed here before.

FRANK.

Jack's undecided.   Say, *formose puer*,
  Bent in a dream above the " water wan,"
Shall we row higher, for the reeds are fewer,
    There by the pollards, where you see the
    swan ?

JACK.

Hist! That's a pike. Look—nose against the
    river
  Gaunt as a wolf,—the sly old privateer!
Enter a gudgeon. Snap,—a gulp, a shiver;—
  Exit the gudgeon. Let us anchor here.

FRANK (*in the grass*).

Jove, what a day! Black Care upon the
    crupper
  Nods at his post, and slumbers in the sun;
Half of Theocritus, with a touch of Tupper,
  Churns in my head. The frenzy has begun.

LAWRENCE.

Sing to us then. Damœtas in a choker,
  Much out of tune, will edify the rooks.

FRANK.

Sing you again. So musical a croaker
  Surely will draw the fish upon the hooks.

JACK.

Sing while you may.   The beard of manhood
   still is
   Faint on your cheeks, but I, alas ! am old.
Doubtless you yet believe in Amaryllis ;—
   Sing me of Her, whose name may not be
      told.

FRANK.

Listen, O Thames !   His budding beard is
   riper,
   Say—by a week.   Well, Lawrence, shall we
      sing?

LAWRENCE.

Yes, if you will.   But ere I play the piper,
   Let him declare the prize he has to bring.

JACK.

Here then, my Shepherds.   Lo, to him ac-
   counted
   First in the song, a Pipe I will impart ;—
This, my Belovèd, marvellously mounted,
   Amber and foam,—a miracle of art.

LAWRENCE.

Lordly the gift.   O Muse of many numbers,
   Grant me a soft alliterative song !

FRANK.

Me too, O Muse !   And when the Umpire
   slumbers,
   Sting him with gnats a summer evening long.

LAWRENCE.

Not in a cot, begarlanded of spiders,
   Not where the brook traditionally "purls,"—
No, in the Row, supreme among the riders,
   Seek I the gem,—the paragon of girls.

FRANK.

Not in the waste of column and of coping,
   Not in the sham and stucco of a square,—
No, on a June-lawn, to the water sloping,
   Stands she I honour, beautifully fair.

LAWRENCE.

Dark-haired is mine, with splendid tresses
    plaited
  Back from the brows, imperially curled;
Calm as a grand, far-looking Caryatid,
  Holding the roof that covers in a world.

FRANK.

Dark - haired is mine, with breezy ripples
    swinging
  Loose as a vine-branch blowing in the morn;
Eyes like the morning, mouth for ever singing,
  Blithe as a bird new risen from the corn.

LAWRENCE.

Best is the song with the music interwoven:
  Mine's a musician,—musical at heart,—
Throbs to the gathered grieving of Beethoven,
  Sways to the light coquetting of Mozart.

FRANK.

Best? You should hear mine trilling out a
    ballad,
  Queen at a picnic, leader of the glees,
Not too divine to toss you up a salad,
  Great in Sir Roger danced among the trees,

LAWRENCE.

Ah, when the thick night flares with dropping
  torches,
 Ah, when the crush-room empties of the
   swarm,
Pleasant the hand that, in the gusty porches,
 Light as a snow-flake, settles on your arm.

FRANK.

Better the twilight and the cheery chatting,—
 Better the dim, forgotten garden-seat,
Where one may lie, and watch the fingers
  tatting,
 Lounging with Bran or Bevis at her feet.

LAWRENCE.

All worship mine.   Her purity doth hedge her
 Round with so delicate divinity, that men
Stained to the soul with money-bag and ledger,
 Bend to the goddess, manifest again.

FRANK.

None worship mine.   But some, I fancy, love
  her,—
 Cynics to boot.   I know the children run,
Seeing her come, for naught that I discover,
 Save that she brings the summer and the sun.

LAWRENCE.

Mine is a Lady, beautiful and queenly,
  Crowned with a sweet, continual control,
Grandly forbearing, lifting life serenely
  E'en to her own nobility of soul.

FRANK.

Mine is a Woman, kindly beyond measure,
  Fearless in praising, faltering in blame :
Simply devoted to other people's pleasure,—
  Jack's sister Florence,—now you know her
    name.

LAWRENCE.

"Jack's sister Florence !"   Never, Francis,
  never.
  Jack, do you hear ? Why, it was she I meant.
She like the country ! Ah, she's far too clever—

FRANK.

There you are wrong.   I know her down in
  Kent.

LAWRENCE.

You'll get a sunstroke, standing with your head
  bare.
  Sorry to differ.   Jack,—the word's with you.

FRANK.

How is it, Umpire?   Though the motto's
    thread-bare,
  " *Cælum non animum* "—is, I take it, true.

JACK.

" *Souvent femme varie*," as a rule, is truer ;
    Flattered, I'm sure,—but both of you romance.
Happy to further suit of either wooer,
    Merely observing—you haven't got a chance.

LAWRENCE.

Yes.   But the Pipe—

FRANK.

        The Pipe is what we care for,—

JACK.

Well, in this case, I scarcely need explain,
Judgment of mine were indiscreet, and there
    fore,—
    Peace to you both.   The Pipe I shall retain.
1869.

TU QUOQUE

AN IDYLL IN THE CONSERVATORY

*" — romprons-nous,
Ou ne romprons-nous pas ?"*
—LE DÉPIT AMOUREUX.

NELLIE.

IF I were you, when ladies at the play, sir,
   Beckon and nod, a melodrama through,
I would not turn abstractedly away, sir,
   If I were you !

FRANK.

If I were you, when persons I affected,
   Wait for three hours to take me down to Kew
I would, at least, *pretend* I recollected,
   If I were you.

NELLIE.

If I were you, when ladies are so lavish,
  Sir, as to keep me every waltz but two,
I would not dance with *odious* Miss M'Tavish,
  If I were you !

FRANK.

If I were you, who vow you cannot suffer
  Whiff of the best,—the mildest " honey-dew,"
I would not dance with smoke-consuming Puffer
  If I were you !

NELLIE.

If I were you, I would not, sir, be bitter,
  Even to write the " Cynical Review " ;—

FRANK.

No, I should doubtless find flirtation fitter,
  If I were you !

NELLIE.

Really !   You   would !   Why, Frank, you're
    quite delightful,—
  Hot as Othello, and as black of hue ;
Borrow my fan.   I would not look so *frightful*,
    If I were you !

FRANK.

" It is the cause."   I mean your chaperon is
    Bringing some well-curled juvenile.   Adieu !
I shall retire.   I'd spare that poor Adonis,
    If I were you !

NELLIE.

Go, if you will. At once ! And by express, sir
    Where shall it be ?   To China—or Peru ?
Go.   I should leave inquirers my address, sir.
    If I were you !

FRANK.

No, I remain.   To stay and fight a duel
    Seems, on the whole, the proper thing to do ;—
Ah, you are strong,—I would not then be cruel,
    If I were you !

NELLIE.

One does not like one's feelings to be doubted,—

FRANK.

One does not like one's friends to misconstrue,—

NELLIE.

If I confess that I a wee-bit pouted?—

FRANK.

I should admit that I was *piqué*, too.

NELLIE.

Ask me to dance!   I'd say no more about it,
If I were you!

[Waltz—*Exeunt.*

1872.

A DIALOGUE FROM PLATO

" Le temps le mieux employé est celui qu'on perd."
—CLAUDE TILLIER.

I'D "read" three hours.   Both notes and text
   Were fast a mist becoming ;
In bounced a vagrant bee, perplexed,
   And filled the room with humming,

Then out.   The casement's leafage sways,
   And, parted light, discloses
Miss Di., with hat and book,—a maze
   Of muslin mixed with roses.

"You're reading Greek ?"   "I am—and you ?'
   "O, mine's a mere romancer !"
"So Plato is."   "Then read him—do ;
   And I'll read mine in answer."

I read.   " My Plato (Plato, too,—
   That wisdom thus should harden !)
Declares ' blue eyes look doubly blue
   Beneath a Dolly Varden.' "

She smiled.   " My book in turn avers
   (No author's name is stated)
That sometimes those Philosophers
   Are sadly mis-translated."

" But hear,—the next's in stronger style :
   The Cynic School asserted
That two red lips which part and smile
   May not be controverted ! "

She smiled once more—" My book, I find,
   Observes some modern doctors
Would make the Cynics out a kind
   Of album-verse concoctors."

Then I—" Why not ? ' Ephesian law,
   No less than time's tradition,
Enjoined fair speech on all who saw
   DIANA'S apparition.' "

She blushed—this time.   " If Plato's page
   No wiser precept teaches,
Then I'd renounce that doubtful sage,
   And walk to Burnham-beeches."

"Agreed," I said.   " For Socrates
   (I find he too is talking)
Thinks Learning can't remain at ease
   While Beauty goes a-walking."

She read no more.   I leapt the sill :
   The sequel's scarce essential—
Nay, more than this, I hold it still
   Profoundly confidential.

1872.

LOVE IN WINTER

BETWEEN the berried holly-bush
    The Blackbird whistled to the Thrush:
"Which way did bright-eyed Bella go?
Look, Speckle-breast, across the snow,—
Are those her dainty tracks I see,
That wind beside the shrubbery?"

The Throstle pecked the berries still.
"No need for looking, Yellow-bill;
Young Frank was there an hour ago,
Half frozen, waiting in the snow;
His callow beard was white with rime,—
'Tchuck,—'tis a merry pairing-time!"

"What would you?" twittered in the Wren;
"These are the reckless ways of men.
I watched them bill and coo as though
They thought the sign of Spring was snow;
If men but timed their loves as we,
'Twould save this inconsistency."

"Nay, Gossip," chirped the Robin, "nay ;
I like their unreflective way.
Besides, I heard enough to show
Their love is proof against the snow :—
'Why wait,' he said, 'why wait for May,
When love can warm a winter's day?'"
1871.

POT-POURRI

" Si jeunesse savait ?—"

I PLUNGE my hand among the leaves :
(An alien touch but dust perceives,
Nought else supposes ;)
For me those fragrant ruins raise
Clear memory of the vanished days
When they were roses.

" If youth but knew ! "   Ah, " if," in truth ?—
I can recall with what gay youth,
To what light chorus,
Unsobered yet by time or change,
We roamed the many-gabled Grange,
All life before us ;

Braved the old clock-tower's dust and damp,
To catch the dim Arthurian camp
In misty distance ;
Peered at the still-room's sacred stores,
Or rapped at walls for sliding doors
Of feigned existence.

What need had we for thoughts or cares !
The hot sun parched the old parterres
  And "flowerful closes";
We roused the rooks with rounds and glees,
Played hide-and-seek behind the trees,—
  Then plucked these roses.

Louise was one—light, glib Louise,
So freshly freed from school decree
  You scarce could stop her ;
And Bell, the Beauty, unsurprised
At fallen locks that scandalised
  Our dear "Miss Proper" ;—

Shy Ruth, all heart and tenderness,
Who wept—like Chaucer's Prioress,
  When Dash was smitten ;
Who blushed before the mildest men
Yet waxed a very Corday when
  You teased her kitten.

I loved them all.   Bell first and best ;
Louise the next—for days of jest
  Or madcap masking ;

And Ruth, I thought,—why, failing these,
When my High-Mightiness should please,
    She'd come for asking.

.   .   .   .

Louise was grave when last we met ;
Bell's beauty, like a sun, has set ;
    And Ruth, Heaven bless her,
Ruth that I wooed,—and wooed in vain,—
Has gone where neither grief nor pain
    Can now distress her.
1873.

DOROTHY

A REVERIE SUGGESTED BY THE NAME UPON A PANE

SHE then must once have looked, as I
   Look now, across the level rye,
Past Church and Manor-house, and seen,
As now I see, the village green,
The bridge, and Walton's river—she
Whose old-world name was "Dorothy."

The swallows must have twittered, too,
Above her head ; the roses blew
Below, no doubt,—and, sure, the South
Crept up the wall and kissed her mouth,—
That wistful mouth, which comes to me
Linked with her name of Dorothy.

What was she like ?   I picture her
Unmeet for uncouth worshipper ;—
Soft,—pensive,—far too subtly graced
To suit the blunt bucolic taste,
Whose crude perception could but see
" Ma'am Fine-airs " in " Miss Dorothy."

How not? She loved, maybe, perfume,
Soft textures, lace, a half-lit room ;—
Perchance too candidly preferred
"Clarissa" to a gossip's word ;—
And, for the rest, would seem to be
Or proud, or dull—this Dorothy.

Poor child !—with heart the down-lined nest
Of warmest instincts unconfest,
Soft, callow things that vaguely felt
The breeze caress, the sunlight melt,
But yet, by some obscure decree,
Unwinged from birth ;—poor Dorothy !

Not less I dream her mute desire
To acred churl and booby squire,
Now pale, with timorous eyes that filled
At "twice-told tales" of foxes killed ;—
Now trembling when slow tongues grew free
'Twixt sport, and Port—and Dorothy !

'Twas then she'd seek this nook, and find
Its evening landscape balmy-kind,
And here, where still her gentle name
Lives on the old green glass, would frame

Fond dreams of unfound harmony
'Twixt heart and heart.   Poor Dorothy!

L'ENVOI.

These last I spoke.   Then Florence said,
Below me,—"Dreams?   Delusions, Fred!"
Next, with a pause,—she bent the while
Over a rose, with roguish smile—
"But how disgusted, Sir, you'll be
To hear *I* scrawled that 'Dorothy.'"
1873.

AVICE

"On serait tenté de lui dire, Bonjour, Mademoiselle la Bergeronnette."—Victor Hugo.

THOUGH the voice of modern schools
    Has demurred,
By the dreamy Asian creed
    'Tis averred,
That the souls of men, released
From their bodies when deceased,
Sometimes enter in a beast,—
    Or a bird.

I have watched you long, Avice,
    Watched you so,
I have found your secret out ;
    And I know
That the restless ribboned things,
Where your slope of shoulder springs,
Are but undeveloped wings
    That will grow.

When you enter in a room,
         It is stirred
With the wayward, flashing flight
         Of a bird ;
And you speak—and bring with you
Leaf and sun-ray, bud and blue,
And the wind-breath and the dew,
         At a word.

When you called to me my name,
         Then again
When I heard your single cry
         In the lane,
All the sound was as the ' sweet"
Which the birds to birds repeat
In their thank-song to the heat
         After rain.

When you sang the *Schwalbenlied*,
         'Twas absurd,—
But it seemed no human note
         That I heard ;
For your strain had all the trills,
All the little shakes and stills,
Of the over-song that rills
         From a bird.

You have just their eager, quick
        "*Airs de tête,*"
All their flush and fever-heat
        When elate;
Every bird-like nod and beck,
And a bird's own curve of neck,
When she gives a little peck
        To her mate.

When you left me, only now,
        In that furred,
Puffed, and feathered Polish dress,
        I was spurred
Just to catch you, O my Sweet,
By the bodice trim and neat,—
Just to feel your heart a-beat,
        Like a bird.

Yet, alas! Love's light you deign
        But to wear
As the dew upon your plumes,
        And you care
Not a whit for rest or hush;
But the leaves, the lyric gush,
And the wing-power, and the rush
        Of the air.

So I dare not woo you, Sweet,
                For a day,
Lest I lose you in a flash,
                As I may;
Did I tell you tender things,
You would shake your sudden wings ;—
You would start from him who sings,
                And away.

1868.

THE LOVE-LETTER

"J'ai vu les mœurs de mon tems, et j'ai publié cette lettre."
—LA NOUVELLE HÉLOÏSE.

IF this should fail, why then I scarcely know
  What could succeed.   Here's brilliancy
      (and banter),
Byron *ad lib.*, a chapter of Rousseau ;—
  If this should fail, then *tempora mutantur;*
Style's out of date, and love, as a profession,
Acquires no aid from beauty of expression.

"The men who think as I, I fear, are few,"
  (Cynics would say 'twere well if they were
      fewer) ;
"I am not what I seem,"—(indeed, 'tis true ;
  Though, as a sentiment, it might be newer) ;
"Mine is a soul whose deeper feelings lie
More deep than words"—(as these exemplify).

"I will not say when first your beauty's
        sun
    Illumed my life,"—(it needs imagination);
"For me to see you and to love were
        one,"—
    (This will account for some precipitation);
" Let it suffice that worship more devoted
Ne'er throbbed," et cetera.   The rest is quoted.

"If Love can look with all-prophetic eye,"—
    (Ah, if he could, how many would be
        single !)
"If truly spirit unto spirit cry,"—
    (The ears of some most terribly must tingle !)
"Then I have dreamed you will not turn your
        face."
This next, I think, is more than commonplace.

"Why should we speak, if Love, interpreting,
    Forestall the speech with favour found
        before?
Why should we plead?—it were an idle
        thing,
    If Love himself be Love's ambassador !"
Blot, as I live !   Shall we erase it ?   No ;—
'Twill show we write *currente calamo.*

" My fate,—my fortune, I commit to you,"—
  (In point of fact, the latter's not extensive);
"Without you .I am poor indeed," — (strike
    through,
  'Tis true but crude—'twould make her appre-
    hensive) ;
" My life is yours—I lay it at your feet,"
(Having no choice but Hymen or the Fleet).

" Give me the right to stand within the
    shrine,
  Where never yet my faltering feet intruded ;
Give me the right to call you wholly mine,"—
  (That is, Consols and Three-per-Cents in-
    cluded);
" To guard your rest from every care that
    cankers,—
To keep your life,"—(and balance at your
    banker's)

" Compel me not to long for your reply ;
  Suspense makes havoc with the mind "—
    (and muscles);
" Winged Hope takes flight "—(which means
    that I must fly,
  Default of funds, to Paris or to Brussels);

"I cannot wait !   My own, my queen —
    PRISCILLA !
Write by return."   And *now* for a Manila !

" Miss Blank," at " Blank."   Jemima, let it go ;
    And I, meanwhile, will idle with " Sir Walter";
Stay, let me keep the first rough copy, though—
    'Twill serve again.   There's but the name to
        alter ;
And Love,—that starves,—must knock at every
        portal,
In formâ pauperis.   We are but mortal !
    1872.

A VIRTUOSO

BE seated, pray. "A grave appeal"?
 The sufferers by the war, of course ;
Ah, what a sight for us who feel,—
 This monstrous *mélodrame* of Force !
We, Sir, we connoisseurs, should know,
 On whom its heaviest burden falls ;
Collections shattered at a blow,
 Museums turned to hospitals !

"And worse," you say; "the wide distress !"
 Alas, 'tis true distress exists,
Though, let me add, our worthy Press
 Have no mean skill as colourists ;
Speaking of colour, next your seat
 There hangs a sketch from Vernet's hand ;
Some Moscow fancy, incomplete,
 Yet not indifferently planned ;

Note specially the gray old Guard,
 Who tears his tattered coat to wrap
A closer bandage round the scarred
 And frozen comrade in his lap ;—
But, as regards the present war,—
 Now don't you think our pride of pence
Goes—may I say it?—somewhat far
 For objects of benevolence?

You hesitate.   For my part, I—
 Though ranking Paris next to Rome,
Æsthetically—still reply
 That "Charity begins at Home,"
The words remind me.   Did you catch
 My so-named "Hunt"?   The girl's a gem ;
And look how those lean rascals snatch
 The pile of scraps she brings to them !

"But your appeal's for home,"—you say,—
 "For home, and English poor !"   Indeed !
I thought Philanthropy to-day
 Was blind to mere domestic need—
However sore—Yet though one grants
 That home should have the foremost claims,
At least these Continental wants
 Assume intelligible names ;

While here with us—Ah ! who could hope
  To verify the varied pleas,
Or from his private means to cope
  With all our shrill necessities !
Impossible ! One might as well
  Attempt comparison of creeds :
Or fill that huge Malayan shell
  With these half-dozen Indian beads.

Moreover, add that every one
  So well exalts his pet distress,
'Tis—Give to all, or give to none,
  If you'd avoid invidiousness.
Your case, I feel, is sad as A.'s,
  The same applies to B.'s and C.'s ;
By my selection I should raise
  An alphabet of rivalries ;

And life is short,—I see you look
  At yonder dish, a priceless bit ;
You'll find it etched in Jacquemart's book,
  They say that Raphael painted it ;—
And life is short, you understand ;
  So, if I only hold you out
An open though an empty hand,
  Why, you'll forgive me, I've no doubt.

Nay, do not rise. You seem amused ;
    One can but be consistent, Sir !
'Twas on these grounds I just refused
    Some gushing lady-almoner,—
Believe me, on these very grounds.
    Good-bye, then. Ah, a rarity !
That cost me quite three hundred pounds,—
    That Dürer figure,—" Charity."

1871.

TO Q. H. F.

SUGGESTED BY A CHAPTER IN SIR THEODORE
MARTIN'S "HORACE"

("ANCIENT CLASSICS FOR ENGLISH READERS")

" HORATIUS FLACCUS, B.C. 8,"
　　There's not a doubt about the date,—
　　　　You're dead and buried :
As you observed, the seasons roll ;
And cross the Styx full many a soul
　　　　Has Charon ferried,
Since, mourned of men and Muses nine,
They laid you on the Esquiline.

And that was centuries ago !
You'd think we'd learned enough, I know,
　　　　To help refine us,
Since last you trod the Sacred Street,
And tacked from mortal fear to meet
　　　　The bore Crispinus ;
Or, by your cold Digentia, set
The web of winter birding-net.

Ours is so far-advanced an age !
"Sensation" tales, a classic stage,
      "Commodious" villas !
We boast high art, an Albert Hall,
Australian meats, and men who call
      Their sires gorillas !
We have a thousand things, you see,
Undreamed in your philosophy.

And yet, how strange ! Our "world," to-day,
Tried in the scale, would scarce outweigh
      Your Roman cronies ;
Walk in the Park—you'll seldom fail
To find a Sybaris on the rail
      By Lydia's ponies,
Or hap on Barrus, wigged and stayed,
Ogling some unsuspecting maid.

The great Gargilius, then, behold !
His "long-bow" hunting tales of old
      Are now but duller ;
Fair Neobule too !   Is not
One Hebrus here—from Aldershot ?
      Aha, you colour !
Be wise.   There old Canidia sits ;
No doubt she's tearing you to bits.

And look, dyspeptic, brave, and kind,
Comes dear Mæcenas, half behind
      Terentia's skirting ;
Here's Pyrrha, "golden-haired" at will ;
Prig Damasippus, preaching still ;
      Asterie flirting,—
Radiant, of course.   We'll make her black,—
Ask her when Gyges' ship comes back.

So with the rest.   Who will may trace
Behind the new each elder face
      Defined as clearly ;
Science proceeds, and man stands still ;
Our "world" to-day's as good or ill,—
      As cultured (nearly),—
As yours was, Horace !   You alone,
Unmatched, unmet, we have not known.
1873.

CUPID'S ALLEY

A MORALITY

O, Love's but a dance,
*   Where Time plays the fiddle!*
See the couples advance,—
O, Love's but a dance!
A whisper, a glance,—
*   " Shall we twirl down the middle ? "*
O, Love's but a dance,
*   Where Time plays the fiddle!*

IT runs (so saith my Chronicler)
    Across a smoky City ;—
A Babel filled with buzz and whirr,
    Huge, gloomy, black and gritty ;
Dark-louring looks the hill-side near,
    Dark-yawning looks the valley,—
But here 'tis always fresh and clear,
    For here—is " Cupid's Alley."

And, from an Arbour cool and green
   With aspect down the middle,
An ancient Fiddler, gray and lean,
   Scrapes on an ancient fiddle ;
Alert he seems, but aged enow
   To punt the Stygian galley ;—
With wisp of forelock on his brow,
   He plays—in " Cupid's Alley."

All day he plays,—a single tune !—
   But, by the oddest chances,
Gavotte, or Brawl, or Rigadoon,
   It suits all kinds of dances ;
My Lord may walk a *pas de Cour*
   To Jenny's *pas de Chalet ;*—
The folks who ne'er have danced before,
   Can dance—in " Cupid's Alley."

And here, for ages yet untold,
   Long, long before my ditty,
Came high and low, and young and old,
   From out the crowded City ;
And still to-day they come, they go,
   And just as fancies tally,
They foot it quick, they foot it slow,
   All day—in " Cupid's Alley."

Strange Dance !   'Tis free to Rank and Rags ;
　　Here no distinction flatters ;
Here Riches shakes its money-bags,
　　And Poverty its tatters ;
Church, Army, Navy, Physic, Law ;—
　　Maid, Mistress, Master, Valet ;
Long locks, gray hairs, bald heads, and a',—
　　They bob—in "Cupid's Alley."

Strange pairs !   To laughing, light Fifteen
　　Here capers Prudence thrifty ;
Here Prodigal leads down the green
　　A blushing Maid of fifty ;
Some treat it as a serious thing,
　　And some but shilly-shally ;
And some have danced without the ring
　　(Ah me !)—in "Cupid's Alley."

And sometimes one to one will dance,
　　And think of one behind her ;
And one by one will stand, perchance,
　　Yet look all ways to find her ;
Some seek a partner with a sigh,
　　Some win him with a sally ;
And some, they know not how nor why,
　　Strange fate !—of " Cupid's Alley."

And some will dance an age or so
  Who came for half a minute ;
And some, who like the game, will go
  Before they well begin it ;
And some will vow they're "danced to death,"
  Who (somehow) always rally ;
Strange cures are wrought (mine Author saith),
  Strange cures !—in "Cupid's Alley."

It may be one will dance to-day,
  And dance no more to-morrow ;
It may be one will steal away
  And nurse a life-long sorrow ;
What then ? The rest advance, evade,
  Unite, dispart, and dally,
Re-set, coquet, and gallopade,
  Not less—in "Cupid's Alley."

For till that City's wheel-work vast
  And shuddering beams shall crumble ;—
And till that Fiddler lean at last
  From off his seat shall tumble ;—
Till then (the Civic records say),
  This quaint, fantastic *ballet*
Of Go and Stay, of Yea and Nay,
  Must last—in "Cupid's Alley."
  1876.

THE IDYLL OF THE CARP

(The SCENE is in a garden,—where you please,
　So that it lie in France, and have withal
Its gray-stoned pond beneath the arching trees,
　And Triton huge, with moss for coronal.
A PRINCESS,—feeding fish.　To her DENISE.)

THE PRINCESS.

THESE, DENISE, are my Suitors !

DENISE.

Where?

THE PRINCESS.

These fish.

I feed them daily here at morn and night
With crumbs of favour,—scraps of graciousness,
Not meant, indeed, to mean the thing they wish,
But serving just to edge an appetite.

(*Throwing bread.*)

Make haste, *Messieurs !*　Make haste, then !
　Hurry.　See,—
See how they swim !　Would you not say,
　confess,
Some crowd of Courtiers in the audience hall,
When the King comes?

DENISE.

You're jesting !

THE PRINCESS.

Not at all.

Watch but the great one yonder !   There's the
    Duke ;—

Those gill-marks mean his Order of St. Luke ;

Those old skin-stains his boasted quarterings.

Look what a swirl and roll of tide he brings ;

Have you not marked him thus, with crest in air,

Breathing disdain, descend the palace-stair ?

You surely have, DENISE

DENISE.

I think I have.

But there's another, older and more grave,—

The one that wears the round patch on the
    throat,

And swims with such slow fins.   Is he of note ?

THE PRINCESS.

Why that's my good *chambellan*—with his seal.

A kind old man !—he carves me orange-peel

In quaint devices at refection-hours,

Equips my sweet-pouch, brings me morning
    flowers,

Or chirrups madrigals with old, sweet words,
Such as men loved when people wooed like
    birds
And spoke the true note first.   No suitor he,
Yet loves me too,—though in a graybeard's key.

DENISE.

Look, Madam, look !—a fish without a stain !
O speckless, fleckless fish !   Who is it, pray,
That bears him so discreetly ?

THE PRINCESS.

> FONTENAY.

You know him not ?   My prince of shining
    locks !
My pearl !—my Phœnix !—my pomander-box !
He loves not Me, alas !   The man's too vain !
He loves his doublet better than my suit,—
His graces than my favours.   Still his sash
Sits not amiss, and he can touch the lute
Not wholly out of tune—

DENISE.

> Ai ! what a splash !

Who is it comes with such a sudden dash
Plump i' the midst, and leaps the others clear ?

THE PRINCESS.

Ho ! for a trumpet !   Let the bells be rung !
Baron of *Sans-terre*, Lord of *Prés-en-Cieux*,
Vidame of *Vol-au-Vent—"et aultres lieux!"*
Bah !   How I hate his Gasconading tongue !
Why, that's my bragging Bravo-Musketeer—
My carpet cut-throat, valiant by a scar
Got in a brawl that stands for Spanish war :—
His very life's a splash !

DENISE.

          I'd rather wear
E'en such a pinched and melancholy air,
As his, — that motley one, — who keeps the
    wall,
And hugs his own lean thoughts for carnival.

THE PRINCESS.

My frankest wooer !   Thus *his* love he tells
To mournful moving of his cap and bells.
He loves me (so he saith) as Slaves the
    Free,—
As Cowards War,—as young Maids Constancy.
Item, he loves me as the Hawk the Dove ;
He loves me as the Inquisition Thought !—

Denise.

"He loves?—he loves?" Why all this loving's
　　naught!

The Princess.

And "Naught (quoth Jacquot) makes the sum
　　of Love!"

Denise.

The cynic knave! How call you this one
　　here?—
This small shy-looking fish, that hovers near,
And circles, like a cat around a cage,
To snatch the surplus.

The Princess.

　　　　　　Chérubin, the page.
'Tis but a child, yet with that roguish smile,
And those sly looks, the child will make hearts
　　ache
Not five years hence, I prophesy. Meanwhile,
He lives to plague the swans upon the lake,
To steal my comfits, and the monkey's cake.

DENISE.

And these—that swim aside—who may these
    be?

THE PRINCESS.

Those—are two gentlemen of Picardy.
Equal in blood,—of equal bravery :—
D'AURELLES and MAUFRIGNAC.   They hunt
    in pair ;
I mete them morsels with an equal care,
Lest they should eat each other,—or eat Me.

DENISE.

And that—and that—and that?

THE PRINCESS.

                        I name them not.
Those are the crowd who merely think their lot
The lighter by my land.

DENISE.

                        And is there none
More prized than most?   There surely must be
    one,—
A Carp of carps !

THE PRINCESS.

Ah me!—he will not come!
He swims at large,—looks shyly on,—is dumb.
Sometimes, indeed, I think he fain would nibble,
But while he stays with doubts and fears to
    quibble,
Some gilded fop, or mincing courtier-fribble,
Slips smartly in,—and gets the proffered crumb.
He should have all my crumbs—if he'd but ask;
Nay, an he would, it were no hopeless task
To gain a something more. But though he's
    brave,
He's far too proud to be a dangling slave;
And then—he's modest! So . . . he will not
    come!
  1875.

THE SUNDIAL

'TIS an old dial, dark with many a stain ;
    In summer crowned with drifting orchard
        bloom,
Tricked in the autumn with the yellow rain,
    And white in winter like a marble tomb ;

And round about its gray, time-eaten brow
    Lean letters speak—a worn and shattered
        row :
𝕴 am a 𝔖𝔥𝔞𝔡𝔢 : a 𝔖𝔥𝔞𝔡𝔬𝔴𝔢 too arte thou :
    𝕴 marke the 𝔗ime : saye, 𝔊ossip, dost thou soe ?

Here would the ringdoves linger, head to head ;
    And here the snail a silver course would run,
Beating old Time ; and here the peacock spread
    His gold-green glory, shutting out the sun.

The tardy shade moved forward to the noon ;
    Betwixt the paths a dainty Beauty stept,
That swung a flower, and, smiling, hummed a
        tune,—
    Before whose feet a barking spaniel leapt.

O'er her blue dress an endless blossom strayed ;
   About her tendril-curls the sunlight shone ;
And round her train the tiger-lilies swayed,
   Like courtiers bowing till the queen be gone.

She leaned upon the slab a little while,
   Then drew a jewelled pencil from her zone,
Scribbled a something with a frolic smile,
   Folded, inscribed, and niched it in the stone.

The shade slipped on, no swifter than the snail
   There came a second lady to the place,
Dove-eyed, dove-robed, and something wan and
      pale—
   An inner beauty shining from her face.

She, as if listless with a lonely love,
   Straying among the alleys with a book,—
Herrick or Herbert,—watched the circling dove,
   And spied the tiny letter in the nook.

Then, like to one who confirmation found
   Of some dread secret half-accounted true,—
Who knew what hands and hearts the letter
      bound,
   And argued loving commerce 'twixt the two,—

She bent her fair young forehead on the stone;
　The dark shade gloomed an instant on her
　　head;
And 'twixt her taper-fingers pearled and shone
　The single tear that tear-worn eyes will
　　shed.

The shade slipped onward to the falling gloom;
　There came a soldier gallant in her stead,
Swinging a beaver with a swaling plume,
　　A ribboned love-lock rippling from his
　　　head;

Blue-eyed, frank-faced, with clear and open
　　brow,
　Scar-seamed a little, as the women love;
So kindly fronted that you marvel how
　　The frequent sword-hilt had so frayed his
　　　glove;

Who switched at Psyche plunging in the sun;
　Uncrowned three lilies with a backward
　　swinge;
And standing somewhat widely, like to one
　More used to "Boot and Saddle" than to
　　cringe

As courtiers do, but gentleman withal,
   Took out the note; held it as one who feared
The fragile thing he held would slip and fall;
   Read and re-read, pulling his tawny beard;

Kissed it, I think, and hid it in his breast;
   Laughed softly in a flattered happy way,
Arranged the broidered baldrick on his chest,
   And sauntered past, singing a roundelay.

      .   .   .   .   .

The shade crept forward through the dying
     glow;
   There came no more nor dame nor cavalier;
But for a little time the brass will show
   A small gray spot—the record of a tear.
   1865.

AN UNFINISHED SONG

" Cantat Deo qui vivit Deo."

YES, he was well-nigh gone and near his
    rest,
  The year could not renew him ; nor the cry
Of building nightingales about the nest ;
  Nor that soft freshness of the May-wind's
    sigh,

That fell before the garden scents, and died
  Between the ampler leafage of the trees :
All these he knew not, lying open-eyed,
  Deep in a dream that was not pain nor ease,

But death not yet. Outside a woman talked—
  His wife she was—whose clicking needles
    sped
To faded phrases of complaint that balked
  My rising words of comfort. Overhead,

A cage that hung amid the jasmine stars
   Trembled a little, and a blossom dropped.
Then notes came pouring through the wicker
      bars,
   Climbed half a rapid arc of song, and stopped.

"Is it a thrush?" I asked. "A thrush," she
      said.
   "That was Will's tune. Will taught him that
      before
He left the doorway settle for his bed,
   Sick as you see, and couldn't teach him more.

"He'd bring his Bible here o' nights, would
      Will,
   Following the light, and whiles when it was
      dark
And days were warm, he'd sit there whistling
      still,
   Teaching the bird. He whistled like a lark."

"Jack! Jack!" A joyous flutter stirred the
      cage,
   Shaking the blossoms down. The bird began;
The woman turned again to want and wage,
   And in the inner chamber sighed the man.

How clear the song was ! Musing as I heard,
　My fancies wandered from the droning wife
To sad comparison of man and bird,—
　The broken song, the uncompleted life,

That seemed a broken song ; and of the two,
　My thought a moment deemed the bird more
　　　blest,
That, when the sun shone, sang the notes it
　　　knew,
　Without desire or knowledge of the rest.

Nay, happier man. For him futurity
　Still hides a hope that this his earthly praise
Finds heavenly end, for surely will not He,
　Solver of all, above his Flower of Days,

Teach him the song that no one living knows?
　Let the man die, with that half-chant of his,—
What Now discovers not Hereafter shows,
　And God will surely teach him more than this.

Again the Bird. I turned, and passed along ;
　But Time and Death, Eternity and Change,
Talked with me ever, and the climbing song
　Rose in my hearing, beautiful and strange.
　1871.

THE CRADLE

HOW steadfastly she'd worked at it !
   How lovingly had drest
With all her would-be-mother's wit
   That little rosy nest !

How longingly she'd hung on it !—
   It sometimes seemed, she said,
There lay beneath its coverlet
   A little sleeping head.

He came at last, the tiny guest,
   Ere bleak December fled ;
That rosy nest he never prest . . .
   Her coffin was his bed.

1877.

BEFORE SEDAN

" The dead hand clasped a letter."
—SPECIAL CORRESPONDENCE.

HERE in this leafy place
    Quiet he lies,
Cold, with his sightless face
    Turned to the skies ;
'Tis but another dead ;
All you can say is said.

Carry his body hence,—
    Kings must have slaves :
Kings climb to eminence
    Over men's graves :
So this man's eye is dim ;—
Throw the earth over him.

What was the white you touched,
    There, at his side ?
Paper his hand had clutched
    Tight ere he died ;—
Message or wish, maybe ;—
Smooth the folds out and see.

Hardly the worst of us
    Here could have smiled !—
Only the tremulous
    Words of a child ;—
Prattle, that has for stops
Just a few ruddy drops.

Look.   She is sad to miss
    Morning and night,
His—her dead father's—kiss ;
    Tries to be bright,
Good to mamma, and sweet.
That is all.   " Marguerite."

Ah, if beside the dead
    Slumbered the pain !
Ah, if the hearts that bled
    Slept with the slain !
If the grief died ;—But no ;—
Death will not have it so.

1870.

BEFORE THE CURTAIN

" MISS PEACOCK 's called."   And who
    demurs?
  Not I who write, for certain ;
If praise be due, one sure prefers
That some such face as fresh as hers
    Should come before the curtain.

And yet, most strange to say, I find
    (E'en bards are sometimes prosy)
Her presence here but brings to mind
That undistinguished crowd behind
    For whom life's not so rosy.

The pleased young *premier* led her on,
    But where are all the others?
Where is that nimble servant John?
And where's the comic Uncle gone?
    And where that best of Mothers?

Where is "Sir Lumley Leycester, Bart."?
　　And where the crafty Cousin?—
That man *may* have a kindly heart,
And yet each night ('tis in the part)
　　Must poison half-a-dozen !

Where is the cool Detective,—he
　　Should surely be applauded?
The Lawyer, who refused the fee?—
The Wedding Guests (in number three)?—
　　Why are they all defrauded?

The men who worked the cataract?
　　The plush-clad carpet-lifters?—
Where is the countless host, in fact,
Whose cue is not to speak, but act,—
　　The "supers" and the shifters?

Think what a crowd whom none recall,
　　Unsung,—unpraised,—unpitied ;
Women for whom no bouquets fall,
And men whose names no galleries bawl,
　　The Great unBenefit-ed !

Ah, Reader, ere you turn the page,
   I leave you this for Moral :—
Remember those who tread Life's stage
With weary feet and scantest wage,
   And ne'er a leaf for laurel !

1874.

A SONG OF THE FOUR SEASONS

WHEN Spring comes laughing
　　By vale and hill,
By wind-flower walking
　　And daffodil,—
Sing stars of morning,
　　Sing morning skies,
Sing blue of speedwell,—
　　And my Love's eyes.

When comes the Summer
　　Full-leaved and strong
And gay birds gossip
　　The orchard long,—
Sing hid, sweet honey
　　That no bee sips ;
Sing red, red roses,—
　　And my Love's lips.

When Autumn scatters
　　The leaves again,
And piled sheaves bury
　　The broad-wheeled wain,—

Sing flutes of harvest
  Where men rejoice ;
Sing rounds of reapers,—
  And my Love's voice.

But when comes Winter
  With hail and storm,
And red fire roaring
  And ingle warm,—
Sing first sad going
  Of friends that part ;
Then sing glad meeting,—
  And my Love's heart.

1877.

TO A GREEK GIRL

WITH breath of thyme and bees that hum,
    Across the years you seem to come,—
Across the years with nymph-like head,
And wind-blown brows unfilleted ;
A girlish shape that slips the bud
    In lines of unspoiled symmetry ;
A girlish shape that stirs the blood
    With pulse of Spring, Autonoë !

Where'er you pass,—where'er you go,
I hear the pebbly rillet flow ;
Where'er you go,—where'er you pass,
There comes a gladness on the grass ;
You bring blithe airs where'er you tread,—
    Blithe airs that blow from down and sea ;
You wake in me a Pan not dead,—
    Not wholly dead !—Autonoë !

How sweet with you on some green sod
To wreath the rustic garden-god ;
How sweet beneath the chestnut's shade
With you to weave a basket-braid ;

To watch across the stricken chords
    Your rosy-twinkling fingers flee ;
To woo you in soft woodland words,
    With woodland pipe, Autonoë !

In vain,—in vain !   The years divide :
Where Thamis rolls a murky tide,
I sit and fill my painful reams,
And see you only in my dreams ;--
A vision, like Alcestis, brought
    From under-lands of Memory,--
A dream of Form in days of Thought,—
    A dream,—a dream, Autonoë !

1875.

THE SICK MAN AND THE BIRDS

ÆGROTUS.

SPRING,—art thou come, O Spring!
  I am too sick for words;
How hast thou heart to sing,
  O Spring, with all thy birds?

MERULA.

I sing for joy to see again
The merry leaves along the lane,
  The little bud grown ripe;
And look, my love upon the bough!
Hark, how she calleth to me now,—
          "Pipe! pipe!"

ÆGROTUS.

Ah! weary is the sun:
  Love is an idle thing;
But, Bird, thou restless one,
  What ails thee, wandering?

HIRUNDO.

By shore and sea I come and go
To seek I know not what ; and lo !
  On no man's eaves I sit,
But voices bid me rise once more,
To flit again by sea and shore,—
          Flit ! flit !

ÆGROTUS.

This is Earth's bitter cup :—
  Only to seek, not know.
But Thou, that strivest up,
  Why dost thou carol so ?

ALAUDA.

A secret spirit gifteth me
With song, and wing that lifteth me,—
  A Spirit for whose sake,
Striving amain to reach the sky,
Still to the old dark earth I cry,—
         " Wake ! wake !"

ÆGROTUS.

My hope hath lost its wing.
  Thou, that to night dost call,
How hast thou heart to sing
  Thy tears made musical?

PHILOMELA.

Alas for me! a dry desire
Is all my song,—a waste of fire
That will not fade nor fail;
To me, dim shapes of ancient crime
Moan through the windy ways of time,
          "Wail! wail!"

ÆGROTUS.

This is the sick man's song,—
  Mournful, in sooth, and fit;
Unrest that cries "How long?"—
  And the Night answers it.

1869.

A FLOWER SONG OF ANGIOLA

DOWN where the garden grows,
  Gay as a banner,
Spake to her mate the Rose
  After this manner :—
"We are the first of flowers,
  Plain-land or hilly,
All reds and whites are ours,
  Are they not, Lily ?"

Then to the flowers I spake,—
  "Watch ye my Lady
Gone to the leafy brake,
  Silent and shady ;
When I am near to her,
  Lily, she knows ;
How I am dear to her,
  Look to it, Rose."

Straightway the Blue-bell stooped,
  Paler for pride,
Down where the Violet drooped,
  Shy, at her side :—
"Sweetheart, save me and you,
  Where has the summer kist
Flowers of as fair a hue,—
  Turkis or Amethyst?"

Therewith I laughed aloud,
  Spake on this wise,
"O little flowers so proud,
  Have ye seen eyes
Change through the blue in them,—
  Change till the mere
Loving that grew in them
  Turned to a tear?

"Flowers, ye are bright of hue,
  Delicate, sweet;
Flowers, and the sight of you
  Lightens men's feet;
Yea, but her worth to me,
  Flowerets, even,
Sweetening the earth to me,
  Sweeteneth heaven.

"This, then, O Flowers, I sing ;
    God, when He made ye,
Made yet a fairer thing
    Making my Lady ;—
Fashioned her tenderly,
    Giving all weal to her ;—
Girdle ye slenderly,
    Go to her, kneel to her,—

" Saying, ' He sendeth us,
    He the most dutiful,
Meetly he endeth us,
    Maiden most beautiful !
Let us get rest of you,
    Sweet, in your breast ; —
Die, being prest of you.
    Die, being blest.' "

1871.

THE DYING OF TANNEGUY
DU BOIS

En los nidos de antaño
No hay pájaros hogaño.
—SPANISH PROVERB.

YEA, I am passed away, I think, from this ;
 Nor helps me herb, nor any leechcraft
  here,
But lift me hither the sweet cross to kiss,
 And witness ye, I go without a fear.
Yea, I am sped, and never more shall see,
 As once I dreamed, the show of shield and
  crest,
Gone southward to the fighting by the sea ;—
 There is no bird in any last year's nest!

Yea, with me now all dreams are done, I ween,
 Grown faint and unremembered ; voices call
High up, like misty warders dimly seen
 Moving at morn on some Burgundian wall ;

And all things swim—as when the charger
    stands
    Quivering between the knees, and East and
        West
Are filled with flash of scarves and waving
    hands ;—
    There is no bird in any last year's nest!

Is she a dream I left in Aquitaine?—
    My wife Giselle,—who never spoke a word,
Although I knew her mouth was drawn with
    pain,
    Her eyelids hung with tears; and though I
    heard
The strong sob shake her throat, and saw the
    cord
    Her necklace made about it;—she that prest
To watch me trotting till I reached the ford ;—
    There is no bird in any last year's nest!

Ah ! I had hoped, God wot,—had longed that
    she
    Should watch me from the little-lit tourelle,
Me, coming riding by the windy lea—
    Me, coming back again to her, Giselle;

Yea, I had hoped once more to hear him call,
    The curly-pate, who, rushen lance in rest,
Stormed at the lilies by the orchard wall ;—
    There is no bird in any last year's nest!

But how, my Masters, ye are wrapt in gloom !
    This Death will come, and whom he loves he
        cleaves
Sheer through the steel and leather ; hating
        whom
    He smites in shameful wise behind the
        greaves.
'Tis a fair time with Dennis and the Saints,
    And weary work to age, and want for rest,
When harness groweth heavy, and one faints,
    With no bird left in any last year's nest!

Give ye good hap, then, all.   For me, I lie
    Broken in Christ's sweet hand, with whom
        shall rest
To keep me living, now that I must die ;—
    There is no bird in any last year's nest!
    1869.

THE MOSQUE OF THE CALIPH

UNTO Seyd the vizier spake the Caliph
    Abdallah :—
" Now hearken and hear, I am weary, by Allah !
I am faint with the mere over-running of leisure ;
I will rouse me and rear up a palace to
    Pleasure ! "

To Abdallah the Caliph spake Seyd the vizier :
" All faces grow pale if my Lord draweth near ;
And the breath of his mouth not a mortal shall
    scoff it ;—
They must bend and obey, by the beard of the
    Prophet ! "

Then the Caliph that heard, with becoming
    sedateness,
Drew his hand down *his* beard as he thought of
    his greatness ;
Drained out the last bead of the wine in the
    chalice :
" I have spoken, O Seyd ; I will build it, my
    palace !

"As a drop from the wine where the wine-cup
    hath spilled it,
As a gem from the mine, O my Seyd, I will
    build it ;
Without price, without flaw, it shall stand for a
    token
That the word is a law which the Caliph hath
    spoken ! "

Yet again to the Caliph bent Seyd the vizier :
" Who shall reason or rail if my Lord speaketh
    clear ?
Who shall strive with his might ?   Let my Lord
    live for ever !
He shall choose him a site by the side of the
    river."

Then the Caliph sent forth unto Kür, unto
    Yemen,—
To the South, to the North,—for the skilfullest
    freemen ;
And soon, in a close, where the river breeze
    fanned it,
The basement uprose, as the Caliph had
    planned it.

Now the courses were laid and the corner-piece
    fitted ;
And the butments and set-stones were shapen
    and knitted,
When lo ! on a sudden the Caliph heard frown-
    ing,
That the river had swelled, and the workmen
    were drowning.

Then the Caliph was stirred, and he flushed in
    his ire as
He sent forth his word from Teheran to Shiraz;
And the workmen came new, and the palace,
    built faster,
From the bases up-grew unto arch and pilaster.

And the groinings were traced, and the arch-
    heads were chasen,
When lo ! in hot haste there came flying a
    mason,
For a cupola fallen had whelmed half the work-
    men ;
And Hamet the chief had been slain by the
    Turc'men.

Then the Caliph's beard curled, and he foamed
    in his rage as
Once more his scouts whirled from the Tell to
    the Hedjaz;
"Is my word not my word?" cried the Caliph
    Abdallah;
"I *will* build it up yet . . . *by the aiding of
    Allah!*"

Though he spoke in his haste like King David
    before him,
Yet he felt as he spoke that a something stole
    o'er him;
And his soul grew as glass, and his anger passed
    from it
As the vapours that pass from the Pool of
    Mahomet.

And the doom seemed to hang on the palace no
    longer,
Like a fountain it sprang·when the sources feed
    stronger;
Shaft, turret, and spire leaped upward, di-
    minished,
Like the flames of a fire,—till the palace was
    finished!

Without price, without flaw.   And it lay on the
    azure
Like a diadem dropped from an emperor's
    treasure ;
And the dome of pearl white and the pinnacles
    fleckless,
Flashed back to the light, like the gems in a
    necklace.

So the Caliph looked forth on the turret-tops
    gilded ;
And he said in his pride, " Is my palace not
    builded ?
Who is more great than I that his word can
    avail if
My will is my will,"—said Abdallah the Caliph.

But lo ! with the light he repented his scorning,
For an earthquake had shattered the whole ere
    the morning ;
Of the pearl-coloured dome there was left but a
    ruin,—
But an arch as a home for the ring-dove to
    coo in.

Shaft, turret, and spire—all were tumbled and
    crumbled;
And the soul of the Caliph within him was
    humbled;
And he bowed in the dust :—" There is none
    great but Allah !
I will build Him a Mosque,"—said the Caliph
    Abdallah.

And the Caliph has gone to his fathers for ever,
But the Mosque that he builded shines still by
    the river ;
And the pilgrims up-stream to this day slacken
    sail if
They catch the first gleam of the " Mosque of
    the Caliph."

    1876.

IN THE BELFRY

WRITTEN UNDER RETHEL'S "DEATH, THE FRIEND"

TOLL! Is it night, or daylight yet?
 Somewhere the birds seem singing still,
Though surely now the sun has set.

Toll! But who tolls the Bell once more?
He must have climbed the parapet.
Did I not bar the belfry door?

Who can it be?—the Bernardine,
That wont to pray with me of yore?
No,—for the monk was not so lean.

This must be He who, legend saith,
Comes sometimes with a kindlier mien
And tolls a knell.—This shape is Death!

Good-bye, old Bell! So let it be.
How strangely now I draw my breath!
What is this haze of light I see? . . .
IN MANUS TUAS, DOMINE!

1876.

THE LADIES OF ST. JAMES'S

A PROPER NEW BALLAD OF THE COUNTRY AND THE TOWN

"*Phyllida amo ante alias.*"—VIRG.

THE ladies of St. James's
  Go swinging to the play;
Their footmen run before them,
  With a "Stand by! Clear the way!"
But Phyllida, my Phyllida!
  She takes her buckled shoon,
When we go out a-courting
  Beneath the harvest moon.

The ladies of St. James's
  Wear satin on their backs;
They sit all night at Ombre,
  With candles all of wax:
But Phyllida, my Phyllida!
  She dons her russet gown,
And runs to gather May-dew
  Before the world is down.

The ladies of St. James's !
  They are so fine and fair,
You'd think a box of essences
  Was broken in the air :
But Phyllida, my Phyllida !
  The breath of heath and furze,
When breezes blow at morning,
  Is not so fresh as hers.

The ladies of St. James's !
  They're painted to the eyes ;
Their white it stays for ever,
  Their red it never dies :
But Phyllida, my Phyllida !
  Her colour comes and goes ;
It trembles to a lily,—
  It wavers to a rose.

The ladies of St. James's !
  You scarce can understand
The half of all their speeches,
  Their phrases are so grand :
But Phyllida, my Phyllida !
  Her shy and simple words
Are clear as after rain-drops
  The music of the birds.

The ladies of St. James's !
　They have their fits and freaks ;
They smile on you—for seconds ;
　They frown on you—for weeks :
But Phyllida, my Phyllida !
　Come either storm or shine,
From Shrove-tide unto Shrove-tide,
　Is always true—and mine.

My Phyllida !—my Phyllida !
　I care not though they heap
The hearts of all St. James's,
　And give me all to keep ;
I care not whose the beauties
　Of all the world may be,
For Phyllida—for Phyllida
　Is all the world to me !

1883

THE OLD SEDAN CHAIR

" What's not destroy'd by Time's devouring Hand?
Where's Troy, and where's the May-Pole in the Strand?"
—BRAMSTON'S "ART OF POLITICKS."

IT stands in the stable-yard, under the eaves,
    Propped up by a broom-stick and covered
      with leaves :
It once was the pride of the gay and the fair,
But now 'tis a ruin,—that old Sedan chair !

It is battered and tattered,—it little avails
That once it was lacquered, and glistened with
      nails ;
For its leather is cracked into lozenge and
      square,
Like a canvas by Wilkie,—that old Sedan chair !

See,—here came the bearing-straps ; here were
    the holes
For the poles of the bearers—when once there
    were poles ;
It was cushioned with silk, it was wadded with
    hair,
As the birds have discovered,—that old Sedan
    chair !

" Where's Troy ? " says the poet ! Look,—under
    the seat,
Is a nest with four eggs,—'tis the favoured
    retreat
Of the Muscovy hen, who has hatched, I dare
    swear,
Quite an army of chicks in that old Sedan
    chair !

And yet—Can't you fancy a face in the frame
Of the window,—some high-headed damsel or
    dame,
Be-patched and be-powdered, just set by he
    stair,
While they raise up the lid of that old Sedan
    chair !

Can't you fancy Sir Plume, as beside her he
    stands,
With his ruffles a-droop on his delicate hands,
With his cinnamon coat, with his laced solitaire,
As he lifts her out light from that old Sedan
    chair?

Then it swings away slowly.   Ah, many a league
It has trotted 'twixt sturdy-legged Terence and
    Teague ;
Stout fellows !—but prone, on a question of fare,
To brandish the poles of that old Sedan chair !

It has waited by portals where Garrick ´has
    played ;
It has waited by Heidegger's "Grand Mas-
    querade " ;
For my Lady Codille, for my Lady Bellair,
It has waited—and waited, that old Sedan
    chair !

Oh, the scandals it knows !   Oh, the tales it
    could tell
Of Drum and Ridotto, of Rake and of Belle,—
Of Cock-fight and Levee, and (scarcely more
    rare !)
Of Fête-days at Tyburn, that old Sedan chair !

"*Heu! quantum mutata,*" I say as I go.

It deserves better fate than a stable-yard, though !

We must furbish it up, and dispatch it,—" With Care,"—

To a Fine-Art Museum—that old Sedan chair !

1884.

TO AN INTRUSIVE BUTTERFLY

"Kill not—for Pity's sake—and lest ye slay
The meanest thing upon its upward way."
—FIVE RULES OF BUDDHA.

I WATCH you through the garden walks,
  I watch you float between
The avenues of dahlia stalks,
  And flicker on the green ;
You hover round the garden seat,
  You mount, you waver. Why,—
Why storm us in our still retreat,
  O saffron Butterfly !

Across the room in loops of flight
  I watch you wayward go ;
Dance down a shaft of glancing light,
  Review my books a-row ;
Before the bust you flaunt and flit
  Of "blind Mæonides"—
Ah, trifler, on his lips there lit
  Not butterflies, but bees !

You pause, you poise, you circle up
    Among my old Japan ;
You find a comrade on a cup,
    A friend upon a fan ;
Yet wind anon, a breathing-while,
    Around AMANDA'S brow ;—
Dost dream her then, O Volatile !
    E'en such an one as thou?

Away !   Her thoughts are not as thine.
    A sterner purpose fills
Her steadfast soul with deep design
    Of baby bows and frills ;
What care hath she for worlds without,
    What heed for yellow sun,
Whose endless hopes revolve about
    A planet, *ætat* One.

Away !   Tempt not the best of wives ;
    Let not thy garish wing
Come fluttering our Autumn lives
    With truant dreams of Spring !
Away !   Reseek thy "Flowery Land" ;
    Be Buddha's law obeyed ;
Lest Betty's undiscerning hand
    Should slay . . . a future PRAED !

1882.

THE CURÉ'S PROGRESS

MONSIEUR the Curé down the street
    Comes with his kind old face,—
With his coat worn bare, and his straggling hair,
    And his green umbrella-case.

You may see him pass by the little *" Grande
      Place,"*
    And the tiny *" Hôtel-de-Ville "* ;
He smiles, as he goes, to the *fleuriste* Rose,
    And the *pompier* Théophile.

He turns, as a rule, through the *" Marché"* cool,
    Where the noisy fish-wives call ;
And his compliment pays to the *" Belle Thérèse,"*
    As she knits in her dusky stall.

There's a letter to drop at the locksmith's shop,
    And Toto, the locksmith's niece,
Has jubilant hopes, for the Curé gropes
    In his tails for a *pain d'épice.*

There's a little dispute with a merchant of fruit,
  Who is said to be heterodox,
That will ended be with a "*Ma foi, oui!*"
  And a pinch from the Curé's box.

There is also a word that no one heard
  To the furrier's daughter Lou. ;
And a pale cheek fed with a flickering red,
  And a "*Bon Dieu garde M'sieu!*"

But a grander way for the *Sous-Préfet*,
  And a bow for Ma'am'selle Anne ;
And a mock "off-hat" to the Notary's cat,
  And a nod to the Sacristan :—

For ever through life the Curé goes
  With a smile on his kind old face—
With his coat worn bare, and his straggling hair,
  And his green umbrella-case.
    1878.

TO AN UNKNOWN BUST IN THE BRITISH MUSEUM

" Sermons in stones."

WHO were you once? Could we but guess
    We might perchance more boldly
Define the patient weariness
  That sets your lips so coldly ;
You " lived," we know, for blame and fame ;
  But sure, to friend or foeman,
You bore some more distinctive name
  Than mere " B. C.,"—and " Roman " ?

Your pedestal should help us much.
  Thereon your acts, your title,
(Secure from cold Oblivion's touch !)
  Had doubtless due recital ;
Vain hope !—not even deeds can last !
  That stone, of which you're *minus*,
Maybe with all your virtues past
  Endows . . . a TIGELLINUS !

We seek it not ; we should not find.
　　But still, it needs no magic
To tell you wore, like most mankind,
　　Your comic mask and tragic ;
And held that things were false and true,
　　Felt angry or forgiving,
As step by step you stumbled through
　　This life-long task . . . of living !

You tried the *cul-de-sac* of Thought ;
　　The *montagne Russe* of Pleasure ;
You found the best Ambition brought
　　Was strangely short of measure ;
You watched, at last, the fleet days fly,
　　Till—drowsier and colder—
You felt MERCURIUS loitering by
　　To touch you on the shoulder.

'Twas then (why not ?) the whim would come
　　That howso Time should garble
Those deeds of yours when you were dumb,
　　At least you'd live—in Marble ;
You smiled to think that after days,
　　At least, in Bust or Statue,
(We all have sick-bed dreams !) would gaze,
　　Not quite incurious, at you.

We gaze ; *we* pity you, be sure !
   In truth, Death's worst inaction
Must be less tedious to endure
   Than nameless petrifaction ;
Far better in some nook unknown,
   To sleep for once—and soundly—
Than still survive in wistful stone,
   Forgotten more profoundly !

1879.

MOLLY TREFUSIS

" Now the Graces are four and the Venuses two,
And ten is the number of Muses;
For a Muse and a Grace and a Venus are you,—
My dear little Molly Trefusis!"

SO he wrote, the old bard of an "old Maga-
zine";
  As a study it not without use is,
If we wonder a moment who she may have
    been,
  This same "little Molly Trefusis!"

She was Cornish. We know that at once by
    the "Tre";
  Then of guessing it scarce an abuse is
If we say that where Bude bellows back to the
    sea
  Was the birthplace of Molly Trefusis.

And she lived in the era of patches and bows,
   Not knowing what rouge or ceruse is ;
For they needed (I trust) but her natural
     rose,
   The lilies of Molly Trefusis.

And I somehow connect her (I frankly admit
   That the evidence hard to produce is)
With BATH in its hey-day of Fashion and
     Wit,—
   This dangerous Molly Trefusis.

I fancy her, radiant in ribbon and knot,
   (How charming that old-fashioned puce is !)
All blooming in laces, fal-lals, and what not,
   At the PUMP ROOM,—Miss Molly Trefusis.

I fancy her reigning,—a Beauty,—a Toast,—
   Where BLADUD'S medicinal cruse is ;
And we know that at least of one Bard it could
     boast,—
   The Court of Queen Molly Trefusis.

He says she was " VENUS." I doubt it. Beside,
  (Your rhymer so hopelessly loose is !)
His " little " could scarce be to Venus applied,
  If fitly to Molly Trefusis.

No, no. It was HEBE he had in his mind ;
  And fresh as the handmaid of Zeus is,
And rosy, and rounded, and dimpled—you'll
      find—
  Was certainly Molly Trefusis !

Then he calls her " a MUSE." To the charge I
      reply
  That we all of us know what a Muse is ;
It is something too awful,—too acid,—too dry,—
  For sunny-eyed Molly Trefusis.

But " a GRACE." There I grant he was probably
      right ;
  (The rest but a verse-making ruse is)
It was all that was graceful,—intangible,—
      light,—
  The beauty of Molly Trefusis !

Was she wooed? Who can hesitate much about
    that
  Assuredly more than obtuse is ;
For how could the poet have written so pat
  "*My* dear little Molly Trefusis!"

And was wed? That I think we must plainly
    infer,
  Since of suitors the common excuse is
To take to them Wives. So it happened to her,
  Of course,—"little Molly Trefusis!"

To the Bard? 'Tis unlikely. Apollo, you see,
  In practical matters a goose is ;—
'Twas a Knight of the Shire, and a hunting J.P.,
  Who carried off Molly Trefusis!

And you'll find, I conclude, in the "*Gentleman's
    Mag.*,"
  At the end, where the pick of the news is,
"*On the* (blank) *at 'the Bath,' to Sir Hilary
    Bragg,
  With a Fortune*, MISS MOLLY TREFUSIS."

Thereupon . . . But no farther the student may
    pry,
  Love's temple is dark as Eleusis ;
So here, at the threshold we part, you and I,
  From " dear little Molly Trefusis."
  1878.

THE MILKMAID

A NEW SONG TO AN OLD TUNE

ACROSS the grass I see her pass;
　　She comes with tripping pace,—
A maid I know,—and March winds blow
　　Her hair across her face;—
　　　　With a hey, Dolly! ho, Dolly!
　　　　　Dolly shall be mine,
　　　　Before the spray is white with May,
　　　　　Or blooms the eglantine.

The March winds blow.　I watch her go:
　　Her eye is brown and clear;
Her cheek is brown, and soft as down,
　　(To those who see it near!)—
　　　　With a hey, Dolly! ho, Dolly!
　　　　　Dolly shall be mine,
　　　　Before the spray is white with May,
　　　　　Or blooms the eglantine.

What has she not that those have got,—
    The dames that walk in silk!
If she undo her 'kerchief blue,
    Her neck is white as milk.
        With a hey, Dolly! ho, Dolly!
        Dolly shall be mine,
        Before the spray is white with May,
        Or blooms the eglantine.

Let those who will be proud and chill!
    For me, from June to June,
My Dolly's words are sweet as curds—
    Her laugh is like a tune;—
        With a hey, Dolly! ho, Dolly!
        Dolly shall be mine,
        Before the spray is white with May,
        Or blooms the eglantine.

Break, break to hear, O crocus-spear!
    O tall Lent-lilies flame!
There'll be a bride at Easter-tide,
    And Dolly is her name.
        With a hey, Dolly! ho, Dolly!
        Dolly shall be mine,
        Before the spray is white with May,
        Or blooms the eglantine.

1883.

AN EASTERN APOLOGUE

(TO E. H. P.)

MELIK the Sultán, tired and wan,
Nodded at noon on his diván.

Beside the fountain lingered near
JAMÍL the bard, and the vizier—

Old YÚSUF, sour and hard to please;
Then JAMÍL sang, in words like these.

*Slim is Butheina—slim is she
As boughs of the Aráka tree!*

"Nay," quoth the other, teeth between,
"Lean, if you will,—I call her lean."

*Sweet is Butheina—sweet as wine,
With smiles that like red bubbles shine!*

"True,—by the Prophet!" YÚSUF said.
"She makes men wander in the head!"

Dear is Butheina—ah! more dear
Than all the maidens of Kashmeer!

" Dear," came the answer, quick as thought,
" Dear . . and yet always to be bought."

So JAMÍL ceased.   But still Life's page
Shows diverse unto YOUTH and AGE :

And—be the song of ghouls or gods—
TIME, like the Sultán, sits . . and nods.
1881.

A REVOLUTIONARY RELIC

OLD it is, and worn and battered,
    As I lift it from the stall;
And the leaves are frayed and tattered,
And the pendent sides are shattered,
    Pierced and blackened by a ball.

'Tis the tale of grief and gladness
    Told by sad St. Pierre of yore,
That in front of France's madness
Hangs a strange seductive sadness,
    Grown pathetic evermore.

And a perfume round it hovers,
    Which the pages half reveal,
For a folded corner covers,
Interlaced, two names of lovers,—
    A "Savignac" and "Lucile."

As I read I marvel whether,
  In some pleasant old château,
Once they read this book together,
In the scented summer weather,
  With the shining Loire below?

Nooked—secluded from espial,
  Did Love slip and snare them so,
While the hours danced round the dial
To the sound of flute and viol,
  In that pleasant old château?

Did it happen that no single
  Word of mouth could either speak?
Did the brown and gold hair mingle,
Did the shamed skin thrill and tingle
  To the shock of cheek and cheek?

Did they feel with that first flushing
  Some new sudden power to feel,
Some new inner spring set gushing
At the names together rushing
  Of "Savignac" and "Lucile"?

Did he drop on knee before her—
   "*Son Amour, son Cœur, sa Reine*"—
In his high-flown way adore her,
Urgent, eloquent implore her,
   Plead his pleasure and his pain?

Did she turn with sight swift-dimming,
   And the quivering lip we know,
With the full, slow eyelid brimming,
With the languorous pupil swimming,
   Like the love of Mirabeau?

Stretch her hand from cloudy frilling,
   For his eager lips to press ;
In a flash all fate fulfilling
Did he catch her, trembling, thrilling—
   Crushing life to one caress?

Did they sit in that dim sweetness
   Of attained love's after-calm,
Marking not the world—its meetness,
Marking Time not—nor his fleetness,
   Only happy, palm to palm?

Till at last she,—sunlight smiting
  Red on wrist and cheek and hair,—
Sought the page where love first lighting,
Fixed their fate, and, in this writing,
  Fixed the record of it there.

.   .   .   .   .   .

Did they marry midst the smother,
  Shame and slaughter of it all?
Did she wander like that other
Woful, wistful, wife and mother,
  Round and round his prison wall ;—

Wander wailing, as the plover
  Waileth, wheeleth, desolate,
Heedless of the hawk above her,
While as yet the rushes cover,
  Waning fast, her wounded mate ;—

Wander, till his love's eyes met hers,
  Fixed and wide in their despair?
Did he burst his prison fetters,
Did he write sweet, yearning letters
  "*À Lucile—en Angleterre*"?

Letters where the reader, reading,
  Halts him with a sudden stop,
For he feels a man's heart bleeding,
Draining out its pain's exceeding—
  Half a life, at every drop :

Letters where Love's iteration
  Seems to warble and to rave ;
Letters where the pent sensation
Leaps to lyric exultation,
  Like a song-bird from a grave.

Where, through Passion's wild repeating,
  Peep the Pagan and the Gaul,
Politics and love competing,
Abelard and Cato greeting,
  Rousseau ramping over all.

Yet your critic's right—you waive it,
  Whirled along the fever-flood ;
And its touch of truth shall save it,
And its tender rain shall lave it,
For at least you read *Amavit*,
  Written there in tears of blood.

Did they hunt him to his hiding,
　　Tracking traces in the snow?
Did they tempt him out, confiding,
Shoot him ruthless down, deriding,
　　By the ruined old château?

Left to lie, with thin lips resting
　　Frozen to a smile of scorn,
Just the bitter thought's suggesting,
At this excellent new jesting
　　Of the rabble Devil-born.

Till some "tiger-monkey," finding
　　These few words the covers bear,
Some swift rush of pity blinding
Sent them in the shot-pierced binding
　　"*À Lucile, en Angleterre.*"

.　　　.　　　.　　　.　　　.

Fancies only!   Nought the covers,
　　Nothing more the leaves reveal,
Yet I love it for its lovers,
For the dream that round it hovers
　　Of "Savignac" and "Lucile."

1866.

A GARDEN SONG

(TO W. E. HENLEY)

HERE, in this sequestered close,
    Bloom the hyacinth and rose ;
Here beside the modest stock
Flaunts the flaring hollyhock ;
Here, without a pang, one sees
Ranks, conditions, and degrees.

All the seasons run their race
In this quiet resting place ;
Peach, and apricot, and fig
Here will ripen, and grow big ;
Here is store and overplus,—
More had not Alcinoüs !

Here, in alleys cool and green,
Far ahead the thrush is seen ;
Here along the southern wall
Keeps the bee his festival ;
All is quiet else—afar
Sounds of toil and turmoil are.

Here be shadows large and long ;
Here be spaces meet for song ;
Grant, O garden-god, that I,
Now that none profane is nigh,—
Now that mood and moment please,—
Find the fair Pierides !

1885.

A LEGACY

AH, Postumus, we all must go :
   This keen North-Easter nips my shoulder;
My strength begins to fail ; I know
   You find me older ;

I've made my Will.   Dear, faithful friend—
   My Muse's friend and not my purse's !
Who still would hear and still commend
   My tedious verses,—

How will you live—of these deprived ?
   I've learned your candid mind.   The venal —
The sordid soul had scarce survived
   A test so penal ;

But you—Nay, nay, 'tis so.   The rest
   Are not as you : you hide your merit ;
You, more than all, deserve the best
   True friends inherit ;—

Not gold,—that hearts like yours despise ;
   Not "spacious dirt" (your own expression),
No ; but the rarer, dearer prize—
   The Life's Confession !

You catch my thought ? What ! Can't you
    guess ?
   You, you alone, admired my Cantos ;—
I've left you, P., my whole MS.,
   In three portmanteaus !
   1873.

A FANCY FROM FONTENELLE

*" De mémoires de Roses on n'a point vu
mourir le Jardinier."*

THE Rose in the garden slipped her bud,
  And she laughed in the pride of her
    youthful blood,
As she thought of the Gardener standing
    by—
"He is old,—so old! And he soon must
    die!"

The full Rose waxed in the warm June air,
And she spread and spread till her heart lay
    bare;
And she laughed once more as she heard his
    tread—
"He is older now! He will soon be dead!"

But the breeze of the morning blew, and found
That the leaves of the blown Rose strewed the
    ground;

And he came at noon, that Gardener old,
And he raked them gently under the mould.

And I wove the thing to a random rhyme,
For the Rose is Beauty, the Gardener, Time.
  1885.

THE POET'S SEAT

AN IDYLL OF THE SUBURBS

" *Ille terrarum mihi præter omnes Angulus* RIDET."
—HOR. ii. 6.

IT was an elm-tree root of yore,
  With lordly trunk, before they lopped it,
And weighty, said those five who bore
  Its bulk across the lawn, and dropped it
Not once or twice, before it lay,
  With two young pear-trees to protect it,
Safe where the Poet hoped some day
  The curious pilgrim would inspect it.

He saw him with his Poet's eye,
  The stately Maori, turned from etching
The ruin of St. Paul's, to try
  Some object better worth the sketching :—
He saw him, and it nerved his strength
  What time he hacked and hewed and
    scraped it,
Until the monster grew at length
  The Master-piece to which he shaped it.

To wit—a goodly garden-seat,
  And fit alike for Shah or Sophy,
With shelf for cigarettes complete,
  And one, but lower down, for coffee ;
He planted pansies 'round its foot,—
  "Pansies for thoughts !" and rose and arum ;
The Motto (that he meant to put)
  Was " *Ille angulus terrarum.*"

But " Oh ! the change " (as Milton sings)—
  "The heavy change !" When May departed,
When June with its "delightful things"
  Had come and gone, the rough bark started,—
Began to lose its sylvan brown,
  Grew parched, and powdery, and spotted ;
And, though the Poet nailed it down,
  It still flapped up, and dropped, and rotted.

Nor was this all. 'Twas next the scene
  Of vague (and viscous) vegetations ;
Queer fissures gaped, with oozings green,
  And moist, unsavoury exhalations,—
Faint wafts of wood decayed and sick,
  Till, where he meant to carve his Motto,
Strange leathery fungi sprouted thick,
  And made it like an oyster grotto.

Briefly, it grew a seat of scorn,
　　Bare,—shameless,—till, for fresh disaster,
From end to end, one April morn,
　　'Twas riddled like a pepper caster,—
Drilled like a vellum of old time ;
　　And musing on this final mystery,
The Poet left off scribbling rhyme,
　　And took to studying Natural History.

This was the turning of the tide ;
　　His five-act play is still unwritten ;
The dreams that now his soul divide
　　Are more of Lubbock than of Lytton ;
" *Ballades* " are " verses vain " to him
　　Whose first ambition is to lecture
(So much is man the sport of whim !)
　　On " Insects and their Architecture."
1892.

THE TOYMAN

WITH Verse, is Form the first, or Sense?
      Hereon men waste their Eloquence.

"Sense (cry the one Side),—Sense, of course.
How can you lend your Theme its Force?
How can you be direct and clear,
Concise, and (best of all) sincere,
If you must pen your Strain sublime
In Bonds of Measure and of Rhyme?
Who ever heard true Grief relate
Its heartfelt Woes in 'six' and 'eight'?
Or felt his manly Bosom swell
Beneath a French-made *Villanelle?*
How can your *Mens divinior* sing
Within the Sonnet's scanty Ring,
Where she must chant her Orphic Tale
In just so many Lines, or fail? . . ."

" Form is the first (the Others bawl) ;
If not, why write in Verse at all ?
Why not your throbbing Thoughts expose
(If Verse be such Restraint) in Prose ?
For surely if you speak your Soul
Most freely where there's least Control,
It follows you must speak it best
By Rhyme (or Reason) unreprest.
Blest Hour ! be not delayed too long,
When Britain frees her Slaves of Song ;
And barred no more by Lack of Skill,
The Mob may crowd *Parnassus* Hill ! . . ."

Just at this Point—for you must know,
All this was but the To-and-fro
Of MATT and DICK who played with Thought,
And lingered longer than they ought
(So pleasant 'tis to tap one's Box
And trifle round a Paradox !)—
There came—but I forgot to say,
'Twas in the Mall, the Month was May—
There came a Fellow where they sat,
His Elf-locks peeping through his Hat,
Who bore a Basket.   Straight his Load
He set upon the Ground, and showed
His newest Toy—a Card with Strings.
On this side was a Bird with Wings,

On that, a Cage.   You twirled, and lo !
The Twain were one.

                    Said MATT, " E'en so,
Here's the Solution in a Word :—
Form is the Cage and Sense the Bird.
The Poet twirls them in his Mind,
And wins the Trick with both combined."
  1889.

THE TWO PAINTERS

IN Art some hold Themselves content
     If they but compass what they meant ;
Others prefer, their Purpose gained,
Still to find Something unattained—
Something whereto they vaguely grope
With no more Aid than that of Hope.
Which are the Wiser?   Who shall say !
The prudent Follower of GAY
Declines to speak for either View,
But sets his Fable 'twixt the two.

Once—'twas in good Queen ANNA'S Time—
While yet in this benighted Clime
The GENIUS of the ARTS (now known
On mouldy Pediments alone)
Protected all the Men of Mark,
Two Painters met Her in the Park.

Whether She wore the Robe of Air
Portrayed by VERRIO and LAGUERRE ;
Or, like BELINDA, trod this Earth,
Equipped with Hoop of monstrous Girth,
And armed at every Point for Slaughter
With Essences and Orange-water,
I know not : but it seems that then,
After some talk of Brush and Pen,—
Some chat of Art both High and Low,
Of VAN'S "Goose-Pie" and KNELLER'S
        "*Mot*,"—
The Lady, as a Goddess should,
Bade Them ask of Her what They would.
"Then, Madam, my request," says BRISK,
Giving his *Ramillie* a whisk,
"Is that your Majesty will crown
My humble Efforts with Renown.
Let me, I beg it—Thanks to You—
Be praised for Everything I do,
Whether I paint a Man of Note,
Or only plan a Petticoat."
"Nay," quoth the other, "I confess"
(This One was plainer in his Dress,
And even poorly clad), "for me,
I scorn Your Popularity.
Why should I care to catch at once
The Point of View of every Dunce?

Let me do well, indeed, but find
The Fancy first, the Work behind ;
Nor wholly touch the thing I wanted . . . ."
The Goddess both Petitions granted.

Each in his Way, achieved Success ;
But One grew Great.   And which One?
    Guess.

1882.

AD ROSAM

" Mitte sectari, ROSA *quo locorum*
Sera moretur."—HOR. i. 38.

I HAD a vacant dwelling—
   Where situated, I,
As naught can serve the telling,
   Decline to specify ;—
Enough 'twas neither haunted,
   Entailed, nor out of date ;
I put up " Tenant Wanted,"
   And left the rest to Fate.

Then, Rose, you passed the window,—
   I see you passing yet,—
Ah, what could I within do,
   When, Rose, our glances met !
You snared me, Rose, with ribbons,
   Your rose-mouth made me thrall,
Brief—briefer far than Gibbon's,
   Was my " Decline and Fall."

I heard the summons spoken
  That all hear—king and clown :
You smiled—the ice was broken ;
  You stopped—the bill was down.
How blind we are !   It never
  Occurred to me to seek
If you had come for ever,
  Or only for a week.

The words your voice neglected,
  Seemed written in your eyes ;
The thought your heart protected,
  Your cheek told, missal-wise ;—
I read the rubric plainly
  As any Expert could ;
In short, we dreamed,—insanely,
  As only lovers should.

I broke the tall Œnone,
  That then my chambers graced,
Because she seemed "too bony,"
  To suit your purist taste ;
And you, without vexation,
  May certainly confess
Some graceful approbation,
  Designed *à mon adresse.*

You liked me then, *carina,*—
  You liked me then, I think ;
For your sake gall had been a
  Mere tonic-cup to drink ;
For your sake, bonds were trivial,
  The rack, a *tour-de-force ;*
And banishment, convivial,—
  You coming too, of course.

Then, Rose, a word in jest meant
  Would throw you in a state
That no well-timed investment
  Could quite alleviate ;
Beyond a Paris trousseau
  You prized my smile, I know ;
I, yours—ah, more than Rousseau
  The lip of d'Houdetot.

Then, Rose,—But why pursue it ?
  When Fate begins to frown
Best write the final "*fuit,*"
  And gulp the physic down.
And yet,—and yet, that only,
  The song should end with this :—
You left me,—left me lonely,
  Rosa mutabilis !

Left me, with Time for Mentor,
  (A dreary *tête-à-tête !*)
To pen my " Last Lament," or
  Extemporize to Fate,
In blankest verse disclosing
  My bitterness of mind,—
Which is, I learn, composing
  In cases of the kind.

No, Rose.   Though you refuse me,
  Culture the pang prevents ;
" I am not made "—excuse me—
  " Of so slight elements " ;
I leave to common lovers
  The hemlock or the hood ;
My rarer soul recovers
  In dreams of public good.

The Roses of this nation—
  Or so I understand
From careful computation—
  Exceed the gross demand ;
And, therefore, in civility
  To maids that can't be matched,
No man of sensibility
  Should linger unattached.

So, without further fashion—
   A modern Curtius,
Plunging, from pure compassion,
   To aid the overplus,—
I sit down, sad—not daunted,
   And, in my weeds, begin
A new card—"Tenant Wanted;
   Particulars within."

1869.

TO ONE WHO BIDS ME SING

" The straw is too old to make pipes of."
—DON QUIXOTE.

YOU ask a " many-winter'd " Bard
   Where hides his old vocation?
I'll give—the answer is not hard—
   A classic explanation.

" Immortal " though he be, he still,
   Tithonus-like, grows older,
While She, his Muse of Pindus Hill,
   Still bares a youthful shoulder.

Could that too-sprightly Nymph but leave
   Her ageless grace and beauty,
They might, betwixt them both, achieve
   A hymn *de Senectute;*

But She—She can't grow gray ; and so,
  Her slave, whose hairs are falling,
Must e'en his Doric flute forgo,
  And seek some graver calling,—

Not ill-content to stand aside,—
  To yield to minstrels fitter
His singing-robes, his singing-pride,
  His fancies sweet . . and bitter !

1895

"SAT EST SCRIPSISSE"

(TO EDMUND GOSSE, WITH A COLLECTION
OF ESSAYS)

WHEN You and I have wandered beyond
the reach of call,
And all our Works immortal lie scattered on
the Stall,
It may be some new Reader, in that remoter
age,
Will find this present Volume and listless turn
the page.

For him I speak these verses.   And, Sir (I say
to him),
This Book you see before you,—this masterpiece
of Whim,
Of Wisdom, Learning, Fancy (if you will, please,
attend),—
Was written by its Author, who gave it to his
Friend.

For they had worked together,—been Comrades
    of the Pen;
They had their points at issue, they differed
    now and then;
But both loved Song and Letters, and each had
    close at heart
The hopes, the aspirations, the "dear delays"
    of Art.

And much they talked of Measures, and more
    they talked of Style,
Of Form and "lucid Order," of "labour of the
    File";
And he who wrote the writing, as sheet by
    sheet was penned
(This all was long ago, Sir!), would read it to his
    Friend.

They knew not, nor cared greatly, if they were
    spark or star;
They knew to move is somewhat, although the
    goal be far;
And larger light or lesser, this thing at least is
    clear,
They served the Muses truly,—their service was
    sincere.

This tattered page you see, Sir, this page alone
    remains

(Yes,—fourpence is the lowest!) of all those
    pleasant pains;

And as for him that reads it, and as for him that
    wrote,

No Golden Book enrolls them among its "Names
    of Note."

And yet they had their office.   Though they to-
    day are passed,

They marched in that procession where is no
    first or last ;

Though cold is now their hoping, though they
    no more aspire,

They too had once their ardour—they handed
    on the fire.

   1893 [1892].

ROSE-LEAVES

" Sans peser.—Sans rester."

A KISS.

ROSE kissed me to-day.
  Will she kiss me to-morrow?
Let it be as it may,
Rose kissed me to-day
But the pleasure gives way
  To a savour of sorrow ;—
Rose kissed me to-day,—
  Will she kiss me to-morrow?

CIRCE.

IN the School of Coquettes
  Madam Rose is a scholar :—
O, they fish with all nets
In the School of Coquettes !

When her brooch she forgets
  'Tis to show her new collar;
In the School of Coquettes
  Madam Rose is a scholar!

A TEAR.

THERE'S a tear in her eye,—
  Such a clear little jewel!
What *can* make her cry?
There's a tear in her eye.
" Puck has killed a big fly,—
  And it's *horribly* cruel ; "
There's a tear in her eye,—
  Such a clear little jewel!

A GREEK GIFT.

HERE'S a present for Rose,
  How pleased she is looking!
Is it verse?—is it prose?
Here's a present for Rose!
" *Plats*," " *Entrées*," and " *Rôts*,"—
  Why, it's " Gouffé on Cooking."
Here's a present for Rose,
  How *pleased* she is looking!

" URCEUS EXIT."

I INTENDED an Ode,
   And it turned to a Sonnet.
It began *à la mode*,
I intended an Ode ;
But Rose crossed the road
   In her latest new bonnet ;
I intended an Ode ;
   And it turned to a Sonnet.

1874.

THE WANDERER

L OVE comes back to his vacant dwelling,—
  The old, old Love that we knew or yore!
 We see him stand by the open door,
With his great eyes sad, and his bosom swelling.

He makes as though in our arms repelling,
  He fain would lie as he lay before ;—
 Love comes back to his vacant dwelling,—
  The old, old Love that we knew of yore!

Ah, who shall help us from over-spelling
  That sweet forgotten, forbidden lore!
 E'en as we doubt in our heart once more,
With a rush of tears to our eyelids welling,
Love comes back to his vacant dwelling.

 1880.

TO DAFFODILS

(TO A. J. M.)

O YELLOW flowers by HERRICK sung!
　O yellow flowers that danced and swung
　In WORDSWORTH'S verse, and now to me,
　Unworthy, from this " pleasant lea,"
Laugh back, unchanged and ever young;—

Ah, what a text to us o'erstrung,
O'erwrought, o'erreaching, hoarse of lung,
　You teach by that immortal glee,
　　　O yellow flowers!

We, by the Age's œstrus stung,
Still hunt the New with eager tongue,
　Vexed ever with the Old, but ye,
　What ye have been ye still shall be,
When we are dust the dust among,
　　　O yellow flowers!

　1885.

ON A NANKIN PLATE

" AH me, but it might have been !
      Was there ever so dismal a fate?"—
Quoth the little blue mandarin.

" Such a maid as was never seen !
She passed, tho' I cried to her ' Wait,'—
Ah me, but it might have been !

" I cried, ' O my Flower, my Queen,
Be mine !' 'Twas precipitate,"—
Quoth the little blue mandarin,—

" But then . . . she was just sixteen,—
Long-eyed,—as a lily straight,—
Ah me, but it might have been !

" As it was, from her palankeen,
She laughed—' You're a week too late !'"
(Quoth the little blue mandarin.)

" That is why, in a mist of spleen,
I mourn on this Nankin Plate.
Ah me, but it might have been !"—
Quoth the little blue mandarin.

1883.

ON A FAN THAT BELONGED TO
THE MARQUISE DE POMPADOUR

CHICKEN-SKIN, delicate, white,
    Painted by Carlo Vanloo,
Loves in a riot of light,
    Roses and vaporous blue;
    Hark to the dainty *frou-frou!*
Picture above, if you can,
    Eyes that could melt as the dew,—
This was the Pompadour's fan!

See how they rise at the sight,
    Thronging the *Œil de Bœuf* through,
Courtiers as butterflies bright,
    Beauties that Fragonard drew,
    Talon-rouge, falbala, queue,
Cardinal, Duke,—to a man,
    Eager to sigh or to sue,—
This was the Pompadour's fan!

Ah, but things more than polite
   Hung on this toy, *voyez-vous !*
Matters of state and of might,
   Things that great ministers do ;
   Things that, maybe, overthrew
Those in whose brains they began ;
   Here was the sign and the cue,—
This was the Pompadour's fan !

ENVOY.

WHERE are the secrets it knew ?
   Weavings of plot and of plan ?
—But where is the Pompadour, too ?
This was the Pompadour's *Fan !*

1878.

A BALLAD TO QUEEN ELIZABETH

of the Spanish Armada

KING PHILIP had vaunted his claims;
  He had sworn for a year he would sack us;
With an army of heathenish names
  He was coming to fagot and stack us;
  Like the thieves of the sea he would track us,
And shatter our ships on the main;
  But we had bold Neptune to back us,—
And where are the galleons of Spain?

His carackes were christened of dames
  To the kirtles whereof he would tack us;
With his saints and his gilded stern-frames,
  He had thought like an egg-shell to crack us;
  Now Howard may get to his Flaccus,
And Drake to his Devon again,
  And Hawkins bowl rubbers to Bacchus,—
For where are the galleons of Spain?

Let his Majesty hang to St. James
   The axe that he whetted to hack us ;
He must play at some lustier games
   Or at sea he can hope to out-thwack us ;
   To his mines of Peru he would pack us
To tug at his bullet and chain ;
   Alas ! that his Greatness should lack us !—
But where are the galleons of Spain?

ENVOY.

   GLORIANA ! the Don may attack us
Whenever his stomach be fain ;
   He must reach us before he can rack us, . . .
And where are the galleons of Spain?
   1877.

THE BALLAD OF PROSE AND RHYME

WHEN the ways are heavy with mire and
rut,
  In November fogs, in December snows,
When the North Wind howls, and the doors
      are shut,—
    There is place and enough for the pains of prose;
    But whenever a scent from the whitethorn
      blows,
And the jasmine-stars at the casement climb,
  And a Rosalind-face at the lattice shows,
Then hey!—for the ripple of laughing rhyme!

When the brain gets dry as an empty nut,
  When the reason stands on its squarest toes,
When the mind (like a beard) has a "formal
      cut,"—
    There is place and enough for the pains of
      prose;
    But whenever the May-blood stirs and glows,
And the young year draws to the "golden prime,"
  And Sir Romeo sticks in his ear a rose,—
Then hey!—for the ripple of laughing rhyme!

In a theme where the thoughts have a pedant-
    strut,
  In a changing quarrel of " Ayes " and " Noes,"
In a starched procession of " If " and " But,"—
    There is place and enough for the pains of
      prose ;
  But whenever a soft glance softer grows
And the light hours dance to the trysting-time,
  And the secret is told "that no one knows," —
Then hey !—for the ripple of laughing rhyme !

ENVOY.

IN the work-a-day world,—for its needs and
    woes,
There is place and enough for the pains of prose ;
But whenever the May-bells clash and chime,
Then hey !—for the ripple of laughing rhyme !

   1878.

THE DANCE OF DEATH

(AFTER HOLBEIN)

" Contra vim MORTIS
Non est medicamen in hortis."

HE is the despots' Despot.   All must bide,
　　Later or soon, the message of his might;
Princes and potentates their heads must hide,
Touched by the awful sigil of his right;
Beside the Kaiser he at eve doth wait
And pours a potion in his cup of state;
The stately Queen his bidding must obey;
No keen-eyed Cardinal shall him affray;
And to the Dame that wantoneth he saith—
"Let be, Sweet-heart, to junket and to play."
There is no King more terrible than Death.

The lusty Lord, rejoicing in his pride,
He draweth down; before the armèd Knight
With jingling bridle-rein he still doth ride;
He crosseth the strong Captain in the fight;
The Burgher grave he beckons from debate;
He hales the Abbot by his shaven pate,

Nor for the Abbess' wailing will delay ;
No bawling Mendicant shall say him nay ;
E'en to the pyx the Priest he followeth,
Nor can the Leech his chilling finger stay . .
There is no King more terrible than Death.

All things must bow to him.   And woe betide
The Wine-bibber,—the Roisterer by night ;
Him the feast-master, many bouts defied,
Him 'twixt the pledging and the cup shall
    smite ;
Woe to the Lender at usurious rate,
The hard Rich Man, the hireling Advocate ;
Woe to the Judge that selleth Law for pay ;
Woe to the Thief that like a beast of prey
With creeping tread the traveller harryeth :—
These, in their sin, the sudden sword shall
    slay . .
There is no King more terrible than Death.

He hath no pity,—nor will be denied.
When the low hearth is garnishèd and bright,
Grimly he flingeth the dim portal wide,
And steals the Infant in the Mother's sight ;
He hath no pity for the scorned of fate :—
He spares not Lazarus lying at the gate,

Nay, nor the Blind that stumbleth as he may ;
Nay, the tired Ploughman,—at the sinking ray,—
In the last furrow,—feels an icy breath,
And knows a hand hath turned the team astray .
There is no King more terrible than Death.

He hath no pity.   For the new-made Bride,
Blithe with the promise of her life's delight,
That wanders gladly by her Husband's side,
He with the clatter of his drum doth fright ;
He scares the Virgin at the convent grate ;
The Maid half-won, the Lover passionate ;
He hath no grace for weakness and decay :
The tender Wife, the Widow bent and gray,
The feeble Sire whose footstep faltereth,—
All these he leadeth by the lonely way . .
There is no King more terrible than Death.

ENVOY.

YOUTH, for whose ear and monishing of late,
I sang of Prodigals and lost estate,
Have thou thy joy of living and be gay;
But know not less that there must come a day,—
Aye, and perchance e'en now it hasteneth,—
When thine own heart shall speak to thee and
    say,—
There is no King more terrible than Death.
   1877.

A MADRIGAL

[*Written for* Choral Songs in Honour of Queen Victoria 1899, *and set to music by* Sir HUBERT PARRY.]

WHO can dwell with greatness! Greatness
    is too high;
Flowers are for the meadow, suns are for the
    sky:—
Ah! but there is greatness in this land of ours,
High as is the sunlight, humble as the flowers!

QUEEN, of thee the fable! LADY, thine the fate!
Royal, and yet lowly, lowly, and yet great;—
Great in far dominion, great in bannered years,
Greater still as woman, greatest in thy tears!

    1899.

RANK AND FILE

(SOUTH AFRICA, 1900–1)

O UNDISTINGUISHED Dead!
Whom the bent covers, or the rock-strewn steep
Shows to the stars, for you I mourn,—I weep,
    O undistinguished Dead!

None knows your name.
Blacken'd and blurr'd in the wild battle's brunt
Hotly you fell ... with all your wounds in front:
    This is your fame!

1900.

FOR A CHARITY ANNUAL

(ANGEL-COURT)

IN Angel-Court the sunless air
  Grows faint and sick; to left and right
  The cowering houses shrink from sight,
Huddled and hopeless, eyeless, bare.

Misnamed, you say? For surely rare
  Must be the angel-shapes that light
                    In Angel-Court?

Nay! the Eternities are there.
  Death at the doorway stands to smite;
  Life in its garrets leaps to flight;
And Love has climbed that crumbling stair
                    In Angel-Court.

1901.

THE SONG OF THE SEA WIND

HOW it sings, sings, sings,
  Blowing sharply from the sea-line,
With an edge of salt that stings;
  How it laughs aloud, and passes,
  As it cuts the close cliff-grasses;
    How it sings again, and whistles
    As it shakes the stout sea-thistles—
      How it sings!

How it shrieks, shrieks, shrieks,
  In the crannies of the headland,
In the gashes of the creeks;
  How it shrieks once more, and catches
  Up the yellow foam in patches;
    How it whirls it out and over
    To the corn-field and the clover—
      How it shrieks!

How it roars, roars, roars,
  In the iron under-caverns,
In the hollows of the shores ;
  How it roars anew, and thunders,
  As the strong hull splits and sunders :
    And the spent ship, tempest-driven,
    On the reef lies rent and riven—
      How it roars !

How it wails, wails, wails,
  In the tangle of the wreckage,
In the flapping of the sails ;
  How it sobs away, subsiding,
  Like a tired child after chiding ;
    And across the ground-swell rolling,
    You can hear the bell-buoy tolling—
      How it wails !

1901 [1879].

TO F. M. D.

(WITH A VOLUME OF HERBERT)

I

WHEN I go
    From my place
At your feet,
    Sweet,
All I know
    Of your face
I recall,—
    All;
Being by
    (In the net)
I forget.
    Why?

1885 [1868].

II

Being by,
    I but hear
What you say,—
    Yea,
Naught am I
    But an ear
To the word
    Heard;
Then I go
    And the grace
Of your face
    Know.

TO GEORGE H. BOUGHTON, R.A.

(WITH A VOLUME OF VERSES)

SPRING stirs and wakes by holt and hill:
   In barren copse and bloomless close
  Revives the memory of the rose,
And breaks the yellow daffodil.

Look how the spears of crocus fill
   The ancient hollows of the snows,—
     Spring stirs and wakes!

Yet what to you are months? At will
  For you the season comes or goes;
  We watch the flower that fades and blows,
But on your happy canvas still
     Spring stirs and wakes!

  1885.

ROSE, IN THE HEDGEROW GROWN

ROSE, in the hedgerow grown,
　　Where the scent of the fresh sweet hay
Comes up from the fields new-mown,
You know it—you know it—alone,
　So I gather you here to-day.

For here—was it not here, say?—
That she came by the woodland way,
　And my heart with a hope unknown
　　　　　Rose?

Ah yes!—with her bright hair blown,
　And her eyes like the skies of May,
And her steps like the rose-leaves strown
When the winds in the rose-trees play—
　It was here—O my love!—my own
　　　　　ROSE!

1876.

R. L. S.

IN MEMORIAM

THESE to his Memory.   May the Age
      arriving
        As ours recall
That bravest heart, that gay and gallant striving,
        That laurelled pall!

Blithe and rare spirit!   We who later linger
        By bleaker seas,
Sigh for the touch of the Magician's finger,—
        His golden keys!

  1901.

SURGE ET AMBULA

" ARISE, and walk "—the One Voice said ;
  And lo ! the sinews shrunk and dry
Loosed, and the cripple leaped on high,
Wondering, and bare aloft his bed.

The Age of Miracle is fled.
Who to the halt to-day shall cry—
    "Arise, and walk ! "

Yet though the Power to raise the dead
  Treads earth no more, we still may try
  To smooth the couch where sick men lie,
Whispering—to hopeless heart and head—
    "Arise, and walk ! "

  1904.

THE SIMPLE LIFE

" And 'a babbled of green fields."—SHAKESPEARE-CUM-
THEOBALD.

WHEN the starlings dot the lawn,
    Cheerily we rise at dawn ;
Cheerily, with blameless cup,
Greet the wise world waking up ; —
Ah, they little know of this, —
They of Megalopolis !

Comes the long, still morning when
Work we ply with book and pen ;
Then, —the pure air in our lungs, —
Then " persuasion tips our tongues " ;
Then we write as would, I wis,
Men in Megalopolis !

Next (and not a stroke too soon !)
PHYLLIS spreads the meal of noon,
Simple, frugal, choicely clean,
Gastronomically mean ; —
Appetite our entrée is,
Far from Megalopolis !

Salad in our garden grown,
Endive, beetroot,—all our own ;
Bread,—we saw it made and how ;
Milk and cream,—we know the cow ;
Nothing here of " Force " or " Vis "
As at Megalopolis !

After, surely, there should be,
Somewhere, seats beneath a tree,
Where we—'twixt the curling rings—
Dream of transitory things ;
Chiefly of what people miss
Drowsed in Megalopolis !

Then, before the sunlight wanes,
Comes the lounge along the lanes ;
Comes the rocking shallop tied
By the reedy river-side ;—
Clearer waves the light keel kiss
Than by Megalopolis !

So we speed the golden hours
In this Hermitage of ours
(*Hermits* we are not, believe !
Every Adam has his Eve,
Loved with a serener bliss
Than in Megalopolis):—

So—until the shadows fall:
Then Good Night say each and all;
Sleep secure from smoke and din,
Quiet Conscience tucks us in;
Ah, they nothing know of *this*,—
They of Megalopolis!

(*Thus* URBANUS *to his Wife*
Babbled of The Simple Life.
Then—his glances unawares
Lighting on a List of Shares—
Gulping all his breakfast down,
Bustled, by the Train, to TOWN.)

1905.

THE PASSIONATE PRINTER TO HIS LOVE

(WHOSE NAME IS AMANDA)

[With Apologies to the Shade of Christopher Marlowe.]

COME live with me and be my Dear;
　　And till that happy bond shall lapse
I'll set your Poutings in *Brevier,*
　　Your Praises in the largest CAPS.

There's *Diamond*—'tis for your Eyes;
　　There's *Ruby*—that will match your Lips;
Pearl, for your Teeth; and *Minion*-size
　　To suit your dainty Finger-tips.

In *Nonpareil* I'll put your Face;
　　In *Rubric* shall your Blushes rise;
There is no *Bourgeois* in your *Case*;
　　Your *Form* can never need " *Revise.*"

Your Cheeks seem "*Ready for the Press*";
 Your Laugh as *Clarendon* is clear;
There's more distinction in your Dress
 Than in the oldest *Elzevir*.

So with me live, and with me die;
 And may no "FINIS" e'er intrude
To break into mere "*Printers' Pie*"
 The Type of our Beatitude!

(ERRATUM.—If my suit you flout,
 And choose some happier Youth to wed,
'Tis but to cross AMANDA out,
 And read another name instead.)

    AMANDUS TYPOGRAPHICUS.
1906.

TO MYRTALÉ

(WITH HIS VERSES)

MYRTALÉ, when I am gone
   (Who was once Anacreon),
Lay these annals of my heart
In some secret shrine apart;
Into it put all my sighs,
All my lover's litanies,
All my vows and protestations,
All my jealous accusations,
All my hopes and all my fears,
All the tribute of my tears,—
Let it all be there inurned,
All my passion as it burned;
Label it, when I am gone,
"Ashes of Anacreon."

1906.

A PROEM

(To Mr. Arthur Rackham's edition of *Alice in Wonderland*.)

'TIS two-score years since Carroll's art,
   With topsy-turvy magic,
Sent Alice wandering through a part
   Half-comic and half-tragic.

Enchanting Alice! Black-and-white
   Has made your charm perennial ;
And nought save " Chaos and old Night "
   Can part you now from Tenniel ;

But still you are a Type, and based
   In Truth, like Lear and Hamlet ;
And Types may be re-draped to taste
   In cloth of gold or camlet.

Here comes a fresh Costumier then ;
   That Taste may gain a wrinkle
From him who drew with such deft pen
   The rags of Rip van Winkle.

1908 [1907.]

AN EPITAPH

(FOR A PARISH MAGAZINE)

" On n'y lit aucun nom."—VICTOR HUGO.

HERE sleeps, at last, in narrow bed,
   A man of whom; whate'er is spoken,
This may with certainty be said
   His promises were never broken.

He boasted no high-sounding name,
   Or graced with academic letters;
He paid his way though, all the same,
   And—more than once—forgave his debtors.

He never joined the cry of those
   Who prate about the Public Morals;
But reconciled some private foes,
   And patched up sundry standing quarrels.

It never came within his plan
    To "demonstrate" on Want or Labour;
He strove to serve his fellow-man,
    And did his best to love his neighbour.

When Doubt disturbed his honest soul,
    He found in this his consolation :—
We see a part, and not the whole,
    With only scant illumination.

And this, at least, he felt was sure :—
    To give the sick man's hurt a plaster,
To soothe the pain no art can cure,—
    Was but the bidding of his Master.

So, all unpraised, he ran his race ;
    But we, who watched his life, and knew it,
Thus mark his nameless resting-place,
    Because he died too poor to do it.

1908.

A MILTONIC EXERCISE

(TERCENTENARY, 1608–1908)

" Stops of various Quills."—LYCIDAS.

WHAT need of votive Verse
  To strew thy *Laureat Herse*
With that mix'd *Flora* of th' *Aonian Hill?*
  Or *Mincian* vocall Reed,
  That *Cam* and *Isis* breed,
When thine own Words are burning in us still?

  Bard, Prophet, Archimage!
  In this Cash-cradled Age,
We grate our scrannel Musick, and we dote:
  Where is the Strain unknown,
  Through Bronze or Silver blown,
That thrill'd the Welkin with thy woven Note?

Yes—" we are selfish Men ":
  Yet would we once again
Might see *Sabrina* braid her amber Tire ;
  Or watch the *Comus* Crew
  Sweep down the Glade ; or view
Strange-streamer'd Craft from *Javan* or *Gadire !*

  Or could we catch once more,
  High up, the Clang and Roar
Of Angel Conflict,—Angel Overthrow ;
  Or, with a World begun,
  Behold the young-ray'd Sun
Flame in the Groves where the *Four Rivers* go !

        .   .   .   .

  Ay me, I fondly dream !
  Only the Storm-bird's Scream
Foretells of Tempest in the Days to Come ;
  Nowhere is heard up-climb
  The lofty lyric Rhyme,
And the " God-gifted Organ-voice " is dumb.

  1908.

A SONG OF THE GREENAWAY CHILD

AS I went a-walking on *Lavender Hill*,
   O, I met a Darling in frock and frill;
And she looked at me shyly, with eyes of blue,
"Are you going a-walking? Then take me too!"

So we strolled to the field where the cowslips
   grow,
And we played—and we played for an hour or so;
Then we climbed to the top of the old park wall,
And the Darling she threaded a cowslip ball.

Then we played again, till I said—"My Dear,
This pain in my side, it has grown severe;
I ought to have told you I'm past three score,
And I fear that I scarcely can play any more!"

But the Darling she answered,—"O no! O no!
You must play—you must play.—I shan't let
   you go!"
—And I woke with a start and a sigh of despair
And I found myself safe in my Grandfather's-
   chair!

   1908.

"K. G." (KATE GREENAWAY)

(NOVEMBER 6, 1901)

FAREWELL, kind heart! And if there be
   In that unshored immensity
Child-Angels, they will welcome thee.

Clean-souled, clear-eyed, unspoiled, discreet,
Thou gav'st thy gifts to make Life sweet,—
These shall be flowers about thy feet!

   1902.

"TWO MAIDS UPROSE IN THE SHIMMERING LIGHT"

" Qui gagne bataille
Aura mes amours."—
" Qu'il gagne ou qu'il perde
Les aura toujours."

TWO maids uprose in the shimmering light
  Of the clanging battle-morn ;
And one was tressed like the bird of night,
  And one like the ripening corn.

Then out spoke she with the raven locks,
  And her dark eyes glowed like wine :—
" If he slay the foe, the knight I know,
  He shall win this heart of mine ! "

But softlier she of the yellow hair,
  And her blue eyes 'gan to fill :
" Though he gain or lose, the man I choose,
  He shall be my true love still ! "

  1908.

ELIM

(Exodus xv. 27.)

PALM-TREES and wells they found of yore,
  Who—that Egyptian bondage o'er—
    Had sight betimes of feathering green,
    Of lengthened shadows, and between,
The cool, deep-garnered water-store.

Dear,—dear is Rest by sea and shore:
But dearest to the travel-sore,
    Whose camping-place not yet has been
        Palm-trees and wells!

For such we plead.   Shall we ignore
The long Procession of the Poor,
    Still faring through the night-wind keen,
    With faltering steps, to the Unseen?—
Nay: let us seek for these once more
        Palm-trees and wells!
  1909.

IN MEMORIAM

(FRIDAY, MAY 20, 1910)

" Exstinctus amabitur idem."—Hor. *Epist.* ii. 1. 14.

H E that was King an hour ago
    Is King no more ; and we that bend
Beside the bier, too surely know
    We lose a Friend.

His was no " blood-and-iron " blend
    To write in tears a ruthless reign ;
Rather he strove to make an end
    Of strife and pain.

Rather he strove to heal again
    The half-healed wound, to hide the scar,
To purge away the lingering stain
    Of racial war.

Thus, though no trophies deck his car
  Of captured guns or banners torn,
Men hailed him as they hail a star
    That comes with morn :

A star of brotherhood, not scorn,
  A morn of loosing and release—
A fruitful time of oil and corn—
    An Age of Peace !

Sleep then, O Dead beloved ! and sleep
  As one who, when his course is run,
May yet, in slumber, memory keep
    Of duty done ;

Sleep then, our England's King, as one
  Who knows the lofty aim and pure,
Beyond all din of battles won,
    Must still endure.

1910.

TO HUGH THOMSON

(WITH A COPY OF SIR JOHN GILBERT'S
SHAKESPEARE)

IN Fifty-six, when GILBERT drew
   These brave conceptions, people knew
  Little that we to-day repeat
  (Quoting the prophet in the street)
Of Value, Tone, and Point of View !

Their tastes were plain ; their wants were few ;
They liked red suns and skies of blue . . .
  They were so frankly incomplete
      In Fifty-six !

And yet they prized their GILBERT too—
His Knights and Dames, his ruffling crew,
  Where banners fly, and drums are beat,
  And cloth-of-gold and drugget meet . . .
I was a lad then ! Where were you
      In Fifty-six ?
  1913 [1911].

TO TIME, THE TYRANT

" Ave, Imperator, senectus te salutat."

TIME, in whose kingship is Song,
   What shall I bring to thee now,
Weary of heart and of brow—
Now, that the shadows are long?

Not with the young and the strong
   Numbered am I.   And I bow,
      TIME!

Yet—let me stand in the throng;
   Yet—let me hail and allow
   Youth, that no Combat can cow,
Strength, that is stronger than Wrong,
      TIME!

1911.

FOR THE BLINDED SOLDIERS

WE that look on, with God's goodwill,
　　Have one plain duty to fulfil:
　To drive—by all fair means—afar
　This hideous Juggernaut of War,
And teach the Future not to kill.

But there's a plainer duty still:
We need to meet the instant ill,
　　To heal the wound, to hide the scar—
　　　We that look on!

What timelier task for brain and quill
Than aiding eyes no light can thrill,
　No sight of all good things that are.
　No morning sky, no evening star—
Shall we not help with all our skill,
　　We that look on?

1915.

TO BELGIUM

FOR Right, not Might, you fought. The foe,
   Checked in his wild World-overthrow,
  Ravaged, with his remorseless band,
  Your ancient fanes and peaceful land,
Thinking to crush you at a blow.

You are not crushed, as well we know.
If you are trodden 'tis to grow ;
  Nor can they fail at last who stand
      For Right, not Might !

God speed you, Belgium ! Time will show
How large a debt to you we owe.
  To you—through all reverses grand—
  Men stretch to-day a grateful hand . . .
God speed you still—in weal and woe—
      For Right, not Might.

  1917.

AN ARCTIC EPITAPH

N O grave more nobly graced,
No whiter pall than that which wraps the heads
Of those who sleep where the lone land outspreads
　Its ice-bound waste.

These, Mother, were thy sons,
Brood of thy brood, whose seed by sea and land
Still man to-day, and in days gone have manned
　Our English guns.

No mortal foe defied.
What Nature in her silent holds of snow
Hides from all outer ken, they strove to know,
　And striving—died.

　1917.

ON THE FUTURE OF POETRY

BARDS of the Future! you that come
With striding march, and roll of drum,
What will your newest challenge be
To our prose-bound community?

What magic will you find to stir
The limp and languid listener?
Will it be daring and dramatic?
Will it be frankly democratic?

Will Pegasus return again
In guise of modern aeroplane,
Descending from a cloudless blue?
To drop on us a bomb or two?

I know not.   Far be it from me
To darken dark futurity;
Still less to render more perplexed
The last vagary, or the next.

Leave Pindus Hill for those who list,
Iconoclast or anarchist—
So be it.   "They that break shall pay."
I stand upon the ancient way.

I hold it for a certain thing,
That, blank or rhyming, song must sing;
And more, that what is good for verse,
Need not, by dint of rhyme, grow worse.

I hold that they who deal in rhyme
Must take the standpoint of the time—
But not to catch the public ear,
As mountebank or pulpiteer;

That the old notes are still the new,
If the musician's touch be true—
Nor can the hand that knows its trade,
Achieve the trite and ready-made;

That your first theme is Human Life,
Its hopes and fears, its love and strife—
A theme no custom can efface,
Common, but never commonplace;

For this, beyond all doubt, is plain:
The Truth that pleased will please again,
And move men as in bygone years
When Hector's wife smiled through her tears.

1914 [1913].

THE BALLAD OF THE BEGGAR

THE starlings fly in the windy sky,
   The rabbits run out a-row,
The pheasants stalk in the stubble dry,
As I tramp in the evenglow,—
As I tramp, tramp, tramp, and grow
More weary at every stride,
And think, as the riders pass and go—
If I had a horse to ride!

The Farmer trots by on his roadster high,
The Squire on his pony low;
Young Miss sweeps out from the Park-Gate nigh,
And canters away with her beau :—
They are proud of themselves, I trow,
But couldn't I too show pride?
And couldn't I too cut a dash and show,
If I had a horse to ride.?

The Farmer is four times as fat as I,
The Squire he is blind and slow ;
Young Miss has not nearly so bright an eye
As Bess at the " Barley Mow " ;—
Ah, wouldn't I cry " Gee-hup, Gee-ho,"
And wouldn't I bang his side,
And wouldn't I teach him to gallop it though,
If I had a horse to ride !

ENVOY.

It was only a Beggar that grumbled so,
As his blistered feet he eyed ;
But the cry is a cry that we all of us know—
If I had a horse to ride !

1923.

ALTER EGO

WHERE is the boyish Poet
  Who used with you to write?
Alas! his songs are ended:
  I dug his grave last night.

Beneath a flowering myrtle,
  His face against the East,
I buried him at midnight;
  Without a book or priest.

He had grown older, graver,—
  The iron hand of Time
Had chilled the early laughter
  That rippled in his rhyme.

He had grown graver, sadder,
  Before the darkening years;
His voice, once clear and joyous,
  Took evermore of tears.

What should he do but dwindle,
　　What should he do but go?
He could not sing the summer,
　　He would not sing the snow.

His lyre was carved for pleasure,
　　His lot was cast in pain;
Till this gray world grow brighter,
　　He may not rise again!

So, 'neath a flowering myrtle
　　Without a book or priest,
I buried him at midnight,
　　His face against the East.

1923 [1888].

FOR A CLOSING PAGE

" Never a palinode !"—" Q."

LIFE, like a page unpenned,
　Spreads out its whiteness;
Nothing, from end to end,
　Marring its brightness.

Surely a field to claim
　Steadfast endeavour?
Where one might win a name
　Sounding for ever?

·　·　·　·　·　·　·

Now—to review it all—
　What a prosaic,
Forced, ineffectual,
　Paltry mosaic!

Plans that ne'er found a base;
　Wingless upyearning;
Speed that ne'er won the race;
　Fire without burning;

Doubt never set at rest,
　Stifle or falter it;
Good that was not the best ...
　Yet—would you alter it?

Yet—would you tread again
　All the road over?
Face the old joy and pain—
　Hemlock and clover?
．　　．　　．　　．　　．

Yes.　For it still was good,
　Good to be living;
Buoyant of heart and blood;
　Fighting, forgiving;

Glad for the earth and sky;
　Glad—for mere gladness;
Grateful, one knew not why,
　Even for sadness;

Finding the ray of hope
　Gleam through distresses;
Building a larger scope
　Out from successes;

Blithe to the close, and still
　Tendering ever,
Both for the Good and Ill,
　Thanks to the GIVER.
．　　．　　．　　．　　．

So, though the script is slow,
　Blurred though the line is,
Let the poor record go,
　Onward to Finis.

1913.

IN AFTER DAYS

IN after days when grasses high
  O'er-top the stone where I shall lie,
Though ill or well the world adjust
My slender claim to honoured dust,
I shall not question or reply.

I shall not see the morning sky;
I shall not hear the night-wind sigh;
  I shall be mute, as all men must
    In after days!

But yet, now living, fain were I
That some one then should testify,
  Saying—" He held his pen in trust
  To Art, not serving shame or lust."
Will none?—Then let my memory die
    In after days!

1884.

INDEX OF TITLES

INDEX TO FIRST LINES